FATHER AND SON

Time Lost,
Love Recovered

EDWARD C. SELLNER

AVE MARIA PRESS
Notre Dame, Indiana 46556

Edward C. Sellner is the author of several books including *Wisdom of the Celtic Saints* and *Mentoring: The Ministry of Spiritual Kinship* (Ave Maria Press) as well as numerous journal and magazine articles. He is an associate professor of pastoral theology and spirituality and director of the masters program in theology at the College of Saint Catherine in Saint Paul, Minnesota. He holds his doctorate in theology from the University of Notre Dame.

Editor's Note: The author has chosen to use the designations BCE (Before the Christian Era) and CE (Christian Era) instead of BC and AD.

International Standard Book Number: 0-87793-543-2

Library of Congress Catalog Card Number: 94-79360

Cover design by Elizabeth J. French

Cover photograph by H. Armstrong Roberts

Printed and bound in the United States of America.

In memory of my father.
And for my mother,
Dale, and Marybeth

There is one kind of love which is indissoluble, what no interval of time or space can sever or destroy, and what even death itself cannot part.
—John Cassian

Ask your father, let him teach you.
—Abba Antony

Acknowledgments

I WOULD LIKE TO THANK THE FOLLOWING people who read the manuscript in progress and offered invaluable comments and support: Kate Dayton, Mary Erickson, Gretchen Berg, Barbara Turpin, Kay VanderVort, Ken Schmitz, Judy Jackson, Bea Palmer, Mary Pauluk, and Mary Kaye Medinger. I also appreciated the comments and critique from my students at the College of St. Catherine, who read an early version of my manuscript for a course, "Issues in Pastoral Theology." Special thanks go to Frank Cunningham, my editor at Ave Maria Press, for his encouragement and guidance. No one, except myself, of course, is responsible for the content of this book, but all those mentioned have earned my deepest gratitude. Most of all, I want to thank those who helped my family and me through the darkness of grief after the death of my father.

Table of Contents

Introduction

THIS MEMOIR WAS WRITTEN in the days, weeks, and months following my father's sudden death in July 1991. Within hours of returning from the hospital where we had left Dad's body, I found myself reaching for paper and pen. I wrote because I needed to make sense out of my father's dying, to try to comprehend the enormity of that loss. I also wanted to be attentive to what was happening to my family and me as grief took over our lives. As time passed, I wrote as a way of coming to know Dad better, to let him teach me in his absence what I had not heard while he was alive. Perhaps most of all, I wrote in order to be healed, if possible, of the numbing pain of regret, the anguish of knowing that time had been lost between us that can never be recovered.

My father was a bartender in a number of small towns in North Dakota most of his adult life. He spent a great deal of time listening patiently to other people's stories, often into the early hours of the morning. He told me once, with more weariness in his voice than pride, that he probably heard more confessions than the parish priest. I was too young at the time to pay much attention to that remark. Only when he died did I begin to appreciate what a gift Dad had with all sorts of people—what a good listener he was. For many years there had been a great silence between us, a silence I interpreted as disapproval, rejection, lack of love. I didn't realize that listening was his gift, and that, while I waited for him to open up to me, he was waiting for me to share my story with him.

This book is about my father and me, but in many ways it is about all fathers and sons, those relationships of great complexity, conflict, tenderness, and love. At a time in our culture when so many sons have begun to question their relationship with their fathers, and fathers to wonder how best to "parent" their sons, it is written with the hope that by describing my experiences others will be able to name theirs. In so doing, they may find ways of healing memories and wounds that sometimes may seem unbearable. Such a reconciliation process, it seems, is linked with the acknowledgment of pain as well as the shedding of many tears.

What is described here is my own journey into grief, one that began when I set out to where my dad lay dying; it continued on in the weeks following his burial to places thousands of miles from home. Those travels, planned months before for personal and professional reasons, became, in effect, a journey into the desert where unexorcized demons and ghosts from my past awaited me. At the same time, as I travelled through this land of tears, I unexpectedly began to experience my journey as a form of pilgrimage. Not only did I find myself receiving help from family, friends, mentors, and even strangers along the way, but I found guidance from the very spiritual traditions that I was then researching and writing about: the desert Christians who lived during the third, fourth, and fifth centuries after Christ in Egypt, Syria, and Palestine, and the early Celtic saints of the fifth through ninth centuries who lived in Ireland, England, Scotland, and Wales. Both traditions affirmed the value of having spiritual mentors or guides, whom they called elders or soul friends; both believed that relationships of such intimacy and depth survived death itself. What they helped me realize, and what my own experiences confirmed, was how much my father's life and work were rooted in the same traditions of mentoring, the same values. Most of all, I came to realize how much my father in his dying had become for me a living soul friend.

On one level, then, this book is about the changing geographical landscape as I travelled. On a deeper level, it is about interior changes: what I was learning from my grief about my father, myself, and my own vocation of fatherhood. Obviously, not everyone can travel to foreign lands when a loving parent dies. Nor does everyone find help through the spiritual traditions that helped me in my grief. What each of us can do, must do for ourselves, however, is take time to remember, to recall, and to listen to the voices of our elders, especially our parents. Through this attentive listening we may begin to incorporate into our hearts and lives the spiritual legacies they have left behind.

Everything changes with the death of a parent—the ground shifts, and the landscape is no longer the same. This is the story of my changing landscape, the landscape of my soul. It takes the form of what the ancient Celts called a *caoine*, the cry from the heart raised as we mourn for those loved ones who have preceded us in death. It is about the discovery of light on the other side of darkness, and the realization that the darkness itself is a mysterious dimension of God.

CHAPTER I

The Crow

> Antony and Paul embraced each other. As
> they talked they perceived that a crow had set-
> tled on a branch of the tree, and softly flying
> down, deposited a whole loaf before their
> wondering eyes.
> —Jerome

A FAVORITE STORY OF MINE tells of two desert fathers, Antony and Paul, who lived in Egypt during the fourth century. The two men had never met, but one night Antony, the younger man, has a dream in which he is told to go in search of the older hermit. Antony leaves his cell and travels through the silence of the wilderness, encountering, as he walks, only the scorching heat of the sun by day and ghosts and wild beasts at night. Almost at the point of giving up, Antony finally sees a light from Paul's hermitage shining in the darkness. As he approaches, feeling relieved and happy to have found the man at last, he raises such a din that Paul becomes frightened and refuses to open his door. Antony pleads tearfully with him until finally Paul comes forth, convinced that anyone who comes in tears can be no threat. The two men embrace, greet one another by name, and give thanks to God for bringing them together. As the two men converse, a crow settles on a branch of a nearby tree and then flies down to them, leaving them a loaf of bread. The two men are amazed by this unexpected deed, and when the crow flies away, Paul turns to Antony and says, "Behold God has sent us our dinner, God the merciful,

God the compassionate." The next morning Paul sends Antony on an errand, and, while he is gone, the older man dies. Antony is overcome by grief. Then he has a vision of Paul climbing the steps to heaven, his face and entire body shining as white as snow.

The first time I read this ancient legend by the early church father, St. Jerome, I was drawn to it. I was moved by its depiction of two men's struggle to overcome their distance and distrust, and the lasting ties of friendship between them when they did. Something that I did not realize until after my father's death, however, was the significance of the crow. It appears in the story not only as a bringer of communion to the two desert elders but as a harbinger of the older man's death. Considering my Irish ancestry and my knowledge of Jungian psychology, I might have been more attuned to its presence. After all, my Irish ancestors from County Mayo were Foys, a name that comes from the word *fiach*, "raven." Among the Irish, ravens or crows are frequently seen as harbingers of death. The earliest Celtic priests, the druids, were said to be able to understand the language of ravens and crows. They believed that these black birds had the ability to impart deep secrets from the Otherworld. According to this same tradition, they also often brought with them the *nigredo*, an affliction of soul, a time of darkness, melancholy, grief that, if one is not overcome by it, can lead to transformation.

None of this crossed my mind the day a crow appeared below the window of my study the summer my father died. It had been the summer of strange occurrences, the summer nothing seemed to work. It was also the summer when, besides teaching a college course on Jungian psychology, I was frantically attempting to complete an essay on John Cassian, one of the great storytellers of the desert Christians, for an international conference in Oxford, England. Throughout June electrical outages had darkened the house intermittently, cut off the phone line and, most maddeningly, disabled my computer. An army of electricians, phone workers, and computer technicians traipsed up and down the steps of our old two-story Dutch colonial house on Princeton Avenue in St. Paul. One at a time, they would knock on our door, introduce themselves, and ask what needed to be done.

Then the crow suddenly made its appearance. I heard it one morning as I was beginning to write—a series of short piercing shrieks that became increasingly loud and persistent. At first I attempted to ignore it, but when I could no longer concentrate, I went to look for the source of all the noise. I found it near the bushes in our front yard, where it was evidently trying to hide from danger. An ugly young bird, crippled by a broken wing, it seemed unaware that the more it screeched, the more vulnerable it became. When I attempted to help it (and myself!) by moving it closer to the oak and fir trees, it only shrieked the louder. Finally I gave up and left it where it was, resigned to its presence in our yard. Returning to my study I shut the window, turned on a fan, and hoped that it would eventually go away. Each day, however, for the next three days, it was still there, screeching incessantly, driving me to distraction and bitter words. On the fourth day it was gone, disappearing as suddenly as it had appeared.

Just as disconcerting as these electrical problems and the screeching crow were the inner events that troubled my nights and days. The preceding winter I had had a dream in which I called home, only to be told by a relative whom I could not identify, "I'm so sorry, your dad died today." When I at last understood the person's message, I began to weep, overcome at the realization that I would never see my father again. In this dream I seemed to be watching, observing myself, trying to make out what was happening.

Months after this disturbing dream, in the spring of 1991, I distinctly heard on two separate occasions an inner voice telling me, "Dad will be dead by October." It came from deep within me, and sounded like a person's voice, quiet, yet convincing. Both times I ignored it, my rationality quickly taking over, assuring me that my imagination was playing tricks.

At the time, I interpreted none of these events in any way as premonitions. Only later, after the phone call on that hot July afternoon, did I begin to wonder.

I was in the middle of preparing for an evening class when I heard the phone's sharp, insistent ring. I picked up the receiver and heard the voice of my younger brother, Dale, on the other end. "Eddie, Dad has had a stroke."

"What do you mean?," I asked stupefied, my mind still immersed in the book that I had been reading, not sure even who was on the other end. Then, recognizing who was calling, I argued irrationally, "But Dad was just here—I just talked to him on the phone two days ago."

"No, no," Dale insisted, "Dad's had a stroke—just a while ago!"

"Oh, God!" It finally hit me, and I asked, "What happened?" And then, without pausing, "Is it serious?"

"I don't know," Dale replied, his voice strained. He related how our sister, Marybeth, had called him and said that Dad and Mom had gone to a clinic in Fargo for a medical checkup that morning, and that Dad had had a stroke while waiting to see the doctor. "He's been taken to St. Luke's Hospital," Dale said, "and I'm leaving for there now."

As my brother talked, I tried to make sense of what I was hearing—and to decide what I should do. I thought of my responsibility to my class, and the need for me to be there in this final week of the summer course. I also thought of my father-in-law, who had had a slight stroke the year before and, except for a problem with his vision, seemed to be doing well.

"I don't know what to say, Dale. If it's not that serious I think I should stay here tonight, teach, and come up in the morning. Get back to me when you find out more."

As soon as I hung up the phone, I knew that shock had already taken over and that denial was in place. How could I not go immediately—no matter how slight the stroke might be? It was my place, as oldest son, to be with my parents and family at this time of such uncertainty; nothing was more important than that. I called my wife, JoAnne, at work, and told her of Dale's phone call; then I phoned some people I thought might be able to substitute-teach for me. I started packing frantically while waiting for Dale's next call. Time stopped and stretched endlessly as the agony of not knowing increased. I kept asking myself, "What is happening? Why this delay?"

At last the phone rang again. I heard my brother say, "It's serious. The stroke is massive. Mom says you should come right now."

JoAnne arrived home just as I was leaving. Her face was drawn, her eyes filled with apprehension, mirroring my own. We quickly discussed what had happened, and I assured her that I would call from Fargo as soon as I could. "Tell the boys that I love them," I said as I left the house, "and that they should pray for their grandpa."

It was not until I had gotten through the late afternoon traffic on the far side of the Twin Cities going north that I was overwhelmed with the possibility that my father could die, might in fact be dead already. Tears streamed down my face. As I wiped them with my sleeve and searched for a tissue, I began to bargain with God, pleading for Dad and for all of us: "Don't let him die now, God. Please, he's too young to die." I thought back to my own grandfather's death, years before. "Grandpa John didn't die-until I was in my late twenties," I said aloud; "John is only ten and Daniel six. It wouldn't be fair. I need him, and my sons need him for at least ten more years." Random thoughts, incoherent words, and then a prayer seeking some sort of compromise: "If Dad has to die, let me be with him."

I drove on, trying to concentrate on my driving and to make as much time as possible without attracting the attention of the highway patrol. It was both the longest and shortest trip of my life, through a surrealistic haze of vivid, yet fleeting images. Outside I could see passing cars, cattle grazing, fields of wheat and corn ripening in the stifling heat; in my mind I viewed a succession of scenes from the past, my past with Dad.

The first memory that came to me was of sitting in the cab of a truck with Dad. I was about six years old, and he was delivering gas in his Standard Oil truck. Wherever we went, he would introduce me to people and to a wider world than I could ever have imagined. "This is my son, Eddie," he'd proudly say, and encouraged by him, I would reach out and shake a stranger's hand. Dad knew a lot of people and got along well with them. To some extent he had to, since we seemed to be constantly moving: first, from Minneapolis where I was born and where my parents owned a grocery store until I was four; then to North Dakota for a couple of years in two little towns, Valley City and Edgeley; then to Cambridge, Minnesota, where I went to second grade; then back again to North Dakota for the rest of my grade school years. It was in Edgeley, with a population of about a thousand, that I felt most at home. Dad was a bartender at the time, and in charge of the city-owned liquor store. Before I was in school, I'd sometimes go with Mom on Saturday afternoons, sit in a booth, and watch him with the customers. Sometimes on Sundays, when I was a little older, I'd help him fill the coolers, wash the dirty glasses, and clean the bar. I wasn't all that impressed with the place: the smoke-filled rooms, the loud music, the dirty toilets. But I saw that my father loved his job, laughing with all those strangers. They'd come in, see his welcoming smile, and slap him on the back. Or, if he stepped out for a moment, they would ask or yell for him. Dad was always, it seemed, available.

Besides his customers, I met a lot of farmers who were his friends, especially the summer I was ten years old. Dad took a job surveying land for the government in addition to his other work, and I helped him. While he held one end of the measur-ing-tape, I would take the other and run out through the fields of wheat, sunflowers, or soybeans, desperately hoping not to encounter any wild animals, especially snakes! That same summer he commented that when he retired, he wanted to move to a ranch in Montana or Wyoming to raise sheep. "You and your second wife!" my mother had replied.

By this time my brother Dale had been born, and I was no longer an only child. In a few more years, Marybeth, our sister, joined us. I met more of Dad's friends. There was Fred, a barber in Edgeley, who let me make a few dollars shining shoes on Saturdays provided I kept his barbershop clean. I was in fifth grade at the time, and I learned to recognize a "tightwad"— someone who would come in with mud and usually worse on his boots and pay me the bare minimum, fifty cents, never thinking to tip. Dad encouraged me to "hang in there," despite my lack of enthusiasm, telling me that the experience would be good for "building character." When I was in sixth grade, Dad's friend Bob, the coach of the basketball team, frequently commiserated with my father. I remembered especially the pained look the two of them exchanged after I dribbled the ball down the court in the wrong direction, scoring points for the opposing team. God, how I tried to be a star athlete for Dad's sake, but too often my physical coordination did not match my determination to succeed! There was also Joe, one of Dad's closest friends, who gave me a job one summer pumping gas. I couldn't help noticing that his patience wore a little thin when I'd forget to place the gas caps back on the customers' cars before they drove away.

Others seemed to like and trust Dad. He was surrounded by friends, and once he owned his own bar, he was always bringing someone home for lunch or dinner. Some of his guests came unannounced; some were not all that sober. Dad listened to the secret conflicts and struggles that his customers and friends faced daily. That was one of the strongest memories I had of my father, besides the smile: a look of bone-crushing weariness, standing behind the bar, being hospitable to yet another customer.

I continued driving toward Fargo, my mind filled with memories. Once I was past St. Cloud, the roads became less congested with the vans and pickups that typically crowd

Minnesota highways. Silos and barns appeared more frequently, and from a distance the water towers and church
spires of the small German towns in Stearns County were
visible above the trees. Occasionally fields of golden
sunflowers interrupted the green landscape, and brown cat-
tails could be seen in the ditches where rainwater had
collected. After I passed Fergus Falls the sky darkened as if
it were about to rain. I saw the highway sign directing
travellers west across the Minnesota border to Wahpeton,
North Dakota, and beyond. Thirty miles from Wahpeton was
Wyndmere, the town where Dad had finally bought a tavern
of his own and moved us when I was just out of eighth grade.
I was reminded of the arguments and conflicts between Dad
and me as I grew older, and of his own dark side.

That dark side, of course, had appeared before we moved
to Wyndmere, and my original trust in him was replaced by
fear. I remember, in particular, his anger. He would come after
me, upset over something, and I wouldn't know what to expect
or do. One time, when I was ten or twelve, he became so angry
at my radio's volume that he ran up the stairs, grabbed me,
shook me, and pushed me against the wall. I lost my balance
and tumbled down the stairs.

I developed a wariness with him. I became watchful, attentive to his changing moods, afraid of opening up to him, afraid
of expressing any feelings. Another time—I don't remember
what I had done—he said, "You're going to grow up to be a
bum." Those words stuck. He'd also get angry at my brother
and berate him. Years later, friends would say what a great dad
I had—and I'd think to myself, "You don't know him!"

It also seemed that no matter how hard I tried to please
my father while I was growing up, my efforts were never good
enough. Perhaps much of it had to do with our different
attitudes, interests, and personalities. He liked small towns; I
found them boring. He always had lots of people around him;
I yearned for solitude. Most of all, he loved sports, while I loved
to read, although during grade school and high school I played

all the usual sports: softball, basketball, football, hockey, soccer, and tennis too. I was an Eagle Scout and went to camp every summer. I loved the lakes in northern Minnesota, being close to nature, swimming in the great outdoors. It was just that my enthusiasm for most sports was not exceptionally high, nor was my skill. My real fascination was with books. I couldn't get enough of them.

The very first book I read, one from the Bobbsey Twins series, opened up a whole new world for me: the world of the imagination, the world beyond the confines of my home and the towns in which we lived. I wanted more. I wanted to know about other people, other places, other times. I wanted to travel and see new lands. I would load my bicycle basket up with volumes, large and small, from the Edgeley library, and bring them home, ten or fifteen at a time. I read about Jesus, Moses, and the lives of the saints at a time when my mother was teaching me about them at home and, as a volunteer religion instructor, at church. I read about Abraham Lincoln, his log-cabin days and his accomplishments as President; later in high school, I became an "expert" on the Civil War. I read about Thomas Merton, the Trappist monk whose first book, *The Seven Storey Mountain*, encouraged others to take seriously their own life-story and spirituality. I read about the Kennedy brothers, John and Robert, and the Irish heritage that was theirs and mine. My inner life became populated with the "great ones" who inspired me.

My father didn't seem to understand. He acted as if history and books were a waste of time, as if I were a creature from another planet.

In fourth grade I got my first pair of glasses. As we walked down the street, I asked, "Dad, do you like my new glasses?" I was relieved and overjoyed to be able to see the blackboard in school without needing to sit in the front row. Dad looked at me, frowned, and then said angrily, "They're nothing to be proud of." I remembered that frown. As a child I feared it, but then, as I grew older, I resented, and eventually came to hate it.

When I was in eighth grade Dad announced that we were moving to Wyndmere. I didn't say anything, but I definitely didn't want to leave. My friends were in Edgeley. I was president of my class. I was having fun at parties, dancing to the new rock and roll music, learning the joys of being with the opposite sex. I didn't want to leave the new split-level home my parents had built in which I had my own room—and my own desk. I didn't want to move to a town even smaller than Edgeley, a town where the unpaved main street had a gigantic slough whenever it rained. Nor did I want to move into an old stucco house, small and ugly, in need of repair. But I had no choice.

That first summer I helped Mom paint the rooms. Then I whitewashed the fence near the alley. Alone. In the meantime, Dad proudly put up a wooden sign outside of Wyndmere as soon as he got there: "Ed's Bar and Lounge." In smaller letters, underneath the reference to his bar, appeared the slogan which had come to him, he said, in a moment of inspiration: "Ed Ain't Mad At Nobody!"

I didn't stay in Wyndmere very long. That fall I went away to a seminary in Minnesota to study for the priesthood. The two priests in our parish, Father Hylden and Father Kuhn, were close friends of my parents, as well as certain of the nuns who would stop in to visit at our house. For years, they had encouraged me to consider the possibility of becoming a priest, and I had seriously thought about it since first grade. I was grateful for the mentoring that I received from them and the high ideals they espoused. I loved the stories of the saints Sister Margaret Mary taught to me in summer school. I appreciated the sacred scriptures and the word proclaimed. I wanted to celebrate the ritual of blessing wine and breaking bread. Above all, I was drawn to the mystery of God, a mystery manifest in the changing colors of the liturgical seasons, the smell of beeswax candles and Easter lilies, the ringing or tolling of the bells. By eighth grade going to the seminary made all kinds of sense. Didn't I want to do something worthwhile with my life, to be "somebody," perhaps even to prove to my father—and to myself—that I wouldn't grow up to be a bum? Didn't I want to give my life for others and get a better education too than the one that I'd receive in Wyndmere? Didn't I want to escape the confines of a small town?

I left Wyndmere in early September, aware that I was going against my father's will. He didn't want me to leave at such an early age. He thought that I needed more time, Mother said; that I should wait until I was out of high school before considering a decision of that magnitude. I was too young to understand his concerns. I could only interpret them as yet another sign of how different we were.

One Sunday afternoon before I left for the seminary, Dad asked me to come with him to the bar. I thought he wanted me to help him clean it one last time. But when we got there, he had me sit down on one of the high wooden stools at the bar. He walked behind it and, with his face reflected in the surface, which had been polished to perfection, he asked me what I wanted to drink. Then, after handing me a Coke, out of the blue, he said, "You can be whomever you want to be. You don't have to go away to prove anything to me."

I didn't know what to say, so I didn't say much at all. I told him that I really wanted to be a priest. I didn't know, then, that he was offering me the greatest gift any father can give his son: the freedom to do whatever seems best and the encouragement to find his own calling.

I thought about that conversation with my dad as I got closer to Fargo, how frequently the two of us kept hearing different things whenever we tried to communicate. Throughout my high school and college years I had only returned to Wyndmere on short vacations. Even during the summer months I worked away from home. I spent one summer pumping gas back in Edgeley. Another summer I worked as a camp counselor in northern Minnesota. When I

was in college, and still in the seminary, I worked one summer
in a ghetto in New Orleans and another summer in a barrio in
Bogota, Colombia. When I did return home, older and more
assertive about my identity and convictions, Dad and I often
found ourselves arguing opposite points of view.

A major confrontation came when I returned from Colombia in the late summer of 1968, after the assassination of Robert
Kennedy. As president of the Young Democrats at the college
I had been attending in Fort Wayne, Indiana, I had worked
hard for Kennedy's primary campaign that spring, and I was
devastated when he died. Needless to say, I had strong convictions about the war in Vietnam. Dad and I almost came to
blows over my hair, and even over my glasses, but the real issues
were much deeper, lying below the surface, waiting to explode.

Dad began to lecture me that morning, as he had done on
other occasions, about my wire-rim glasses and shoulder-length
hair. This time he added, "What will the people in town think?"
After years of keeping back my feelings about the town—and
him—something inside me finally broke, and all the turbulent
waters that had built up over a lifetime came flooding out. We
faced off at the breakfast table. This was one argument I was
not going to run from. This was one fight he intended to win.

"I don't give a damn what the people in town think!" I told
him angrily. "I don't give a damn what you think! What do you
know about life? What do you know about anything?"

My father was stunned by my outburst, but his look of
dismay changed almost instantly to hostility—and to stubborn-
ness. "What do *you* know about anything," he asked, "besides
what you read in books?" It was clear that, contrary to the sign,
Ed *was* mad at somebody—me! Mad at my views, my challenging his; mad, perhaps, most of all, for my leaving home when
I did and for being gone so much of the time.

My mother tried to push us away from each other, crying,
"Stop! Stop it! Neither of you mean what you're saying!" But
we did.

Still mourning the death of Kennedy, I was outraged that my own father was defending the war, disgusted that he could be so stubborn, so stupid, so wrong. I saw him as the enemy, representing all that I hated in the country at the time, especially *his* generation sending *my* generation to fight in the jungles of Southeast Asia. Dad obviously saw me with my long hair and wire-rim glasses in the same light. We took the argument to a deeper level.

Shaking my fist at him, I said defiantly, "If I had my choice, you'd never have been my father." To which Dad shot back, "And I wish you'd never been my son."

My mother was sobbing when Dad turned away and left for work, stamping out of the house. I stayed home with plenty of time on my hands to think about what had just happened. It rained that afternoon, just a quick spring shower. As I stood in the doorway, watching the raindrops splash against the sidewalk, I knew that I had finally said what I had felt for so many years, that I wanted a father who was an intellectual, who would talk with me and share my interests in history, politics, and books. Dad perhaps had wanted a son who, like my younger brother, was a star athlete, a hunter, a fisherman. In effect, I wanted him to be more like me while he wanted me to be more like him. That, at least, was the distinct impression that I had received from him. But, I wondered, was it entirely true? I didn't know the answer. The question, however, raised memories of happier times when I was young: the Christmas he bought me an electric train, the time he surprised me with a puppy, and, yes, the rides with him in the Standard Oil truck. I was struck by the realization that I loved this man who was my father, this man whom I really didn't know all that well.

When the rain stopped, I raked up the brown, decaying leaves that had gathered on the lawn over the long, cold winter. Later that day Dad returned from work for supper. Though he turned his eyes from me, I stopped him at the kitchen door with the words, spoken hesitantly, "Dad. Dad, I'm sorry that I hurt you; I want you to know, Dad, that I love you."

He was taken aback, not knowing what to do. Nodding his head slowly, he seemed to accept my apology, although he didn't actually say anything in return. We never referred to the incident again. That explosive argument had cleared the air— for a time. But the memory of those harsh words lingered, with both of us wounded deeply at a place that had much to do with our self-worth and our self-doubt. People smile again, T. S. Eliot says in his poetry, "but the agony abides." I longed to hear him say the words, "I'm sorry" and "I love you too."

As I neared the city of Moorhead, on the Minnesota state line just across from Fargo, the traffic thickened. I looked anxiously at my watch. It was now almost 7 p.m. The dark clouds had parted without any rainfall, and the sun had returned, briefly, to the western sky.

I recalled the progress made between Dad and me as I matured, married, and had two sons of my own. Years before, with the help of others, I had faced the painful fact that I could not be a Roman Catholic priest, for, although I felt called to priesthood, I did not have a vocation to celibacy. Still fascinated with fundamental questions about life and death, church, ministry, and spirituality, still drawn to the mystery of God, I had finished my theological studies at Notre Dame, intent upon being a teacher who would invite others to reflect on the sacred dimensions of their lives. My mother had difficulty, initially, accepting my decision about the priesthood, but Dad did not. He seemed happy for me, almost relieved; happier when I married JoAnne; happier still with the birth of each grandson. My perspective on him began to change as I watched him take each of my sons on his lap, kiss them, and show them the affection that he had once shown me. I was also, of course, affected by my own experience of human limitations. I was learning that nobody is perfect, and that fatherhood, including mine, is full of conflicts, mistakes, and uncertainties.

Dad and I, however, continued to have fights that brought out the worst in each of us. One had occurred on the way back from Notre Dame, where I had just received my doctorate in theology. President Reagan had been there to receive an honorary degree, and Dad and I fought fiercely over the man's politics and policies. Another emotional episode had taken place later, when I had taken my sons and parents to the Black Hills of South Dakota. On the way back Dad told me that he never wanted to take a trip with me again, because "all we ever do is fight." Just recently, in Kensal, the little town west of Fargo where my parents had retired, we fought over where I had parked my car. But that fight had ended differently. I found it difficult to put my finger on it, but something new entered our relationship. The old distance and distrust between us seemed to be receding. This became most evident the last time I saw Dad and Mom, just a week before my brother's phone call.

Mom and Dad had arrived at our house fresh from my father's high school class reunion in Sleepyeye, Minnesota. JoAnne and I had planned a surprise party later that day to celebrate Dad's seventy-fourth birthday. Dad seemed especially happy, surely related to his having seen the old classmates and friends who had elected him, years before, their senior class president. He was oblivious to the brats, buns, and containers of potato salad stuffed in the refrigerator when he went for a beer. All of us drove to JoAnne's parents' house that afternoon to visit, a ruse that allowed the other relatives, some fifty in all, to gather secretly in our backyard.

When we returned, Dad commented on the number of cars parked on the street. I told him that our next-door neighbor was having a party, and he responded, "I didn't know he had so many friends." As I led him around the house to our backyard, Dad stopped suddenly when he saw all the people waiting for him. His smile at the joke about the cars changed to a look of surprise. Then, hidden in the shade of the overhanging lilac bushes by the fence, Dad began to cry as it dawned on him that we had all gathered there *for him*. No one knew what to say. A clumsy silence settled in for a moment as people smiled back at him and, seeing his tears, looked away, embarrassed. His eyes met mine, and I said quietly to him, "Happy birthday, Dad." I'll never forget his look of happiness and gratitude. It was as if he realized, perhaps for the first time, not only how much he was loved by others, but how much I loved him.

As Dad opened gifts, posed for pictures, and talked to people, his face shone with contentment. When everyone had gone, he asked JoAnne if there was any food left. He had not eaten. He had been too engrossed in conversation, opening gifts, and having a thoroughly good time.

The next day, however, was tense. I had to go to a meeting at the college in the morning, and class preparations for that night preoccupied my thoughts. At noon I picked Dad up at our house and drove to a nearby park for a picnic of fried chicken with Mom, JoAnne, and the boys. We spread a blanket on the grass near the lake, quickly devoured the chicken, and then the three generations of Sellner males walked out on the dock and watched some children fishing. It was a beautiful warm summer day with sunlight dancing on the water and a gentle breeze blowing across the lake. Then we drove to an amusement park. The boys rode one ride after another, beneficiaries of their grandparents' generosity. Dad offered to buy me a drink. He and my mother seemed particularly happy that afternoon, sitting at a picnic table near the rides, basking in the pleasant summer weather and their grandsons' laughter. Maybe it was that scene of serenity, that picture of them relaxing with us, but I did not want to go back to the house to prepare class. I resented having to go when I wanted so much just to be there with them. I didn't want to teach that night, either, knowing that my parents were leaving the next day.

That evening, when I got back from class, Dad was sitting in the recliner chair in the family room watching a Twins game. He knew that it was *my* chair, and, as I entered the room, offered to move. I told him to stay where he was. He looked relaxed, and it didn't seem all that important where I sat. When the boys went up to bed, and Mom and JoAnne retired, the two of us continued watching the game together, not saying much, just quietly enjoying it and each other's company.

The following day they left, though Dad seemed unusually hesitant about going. He changed his mind two or three times that morning, telling Mom that they should stay for another day. I told them that they were welcome to stay as long as they wanted, but, because they had plans to meet another aunt and uncle in Duluth that night, they finally decided to go. JoAnne was at work and the boys at daycare. While my parents packed, I stayed upstairs working on my Cassian paper, which had to be delivered in a few short weeks. I justified my absence by telling myself that if I had a regular 9-to-5 job, I wouldn't be in the house anyway. Still, guilt got the best of me, and when I went down to get a cup of fresh coffee and to see how they were doing, Dad appeared irritated with me. He confronted me briefly on the steps with a lecture about my "working too hard." At the time I didn't know what to say or whether he was really serious, but, since he seemed upset, I let him talk. From our last confrontation in Kensal a few months before I had learned that I could listen to him without reacting.

As they were about to leave, I embraced each of them. When I hugged Dad, he accidentally spilled some of the coffee onto the front of his shirt from the cup in my hand. He obviously hadn't seen me holding it. Annoyed at what I perceived to be his clumsiness, I went to the kitchen to get a wet cloth. When I returned, I quickly wiped off the coffee stains, and he and Mom left.

I watched them drive away in the big, white, gas-guzzling Oldsmobile that I had always detested. I felt a great deal of ambivalence. I was relieved to see them go so that I could get back to my writing, *and* I was deeply apprehensive about when and whether I would see them again. When JoAnne returned from work that day, I told her about the coffee incident. "It's the story of our lives—two men always trying to communicate, to express love to each other, and something always gets in the way." I was surprised by her immediate response, "That's not true; you have a good relationship with your dad."

Now, as I drove across the bridge from Moorhead into Fargo, with the sun beginning to set and the dark shadows to lengthen, I was extremely apprehensive. What I remembered distinctly was that last embrace between Dad and me: *my* irritation at his spilling coffee and *his* laughter as I wiped it off his shirt.

CHAPTER II

A Good Man Dying

Abba Isaac and Abba Abraham lived together.
When he came home one day, Abba Abraham
found Abba Isaac in tears. He asked him, "Why
are you weeping?" The other man replied, "Why
should we not weep? For where have we to go?
Our fathers are dead. We are orphans."

ORDINARILY I AM CONFUSED BY CITY TRAFFIC, but this time my car seemed to drive itself straight to the hospital. Tired from the trip and already feeling dazed, I had only to park the car and rush inside. As my eyes adjusted to the light of the lobby, I saw my mother, half-seated, half-rising from a chair to greet me. My sister, Marybeth, and her husband, Jim, were seated beside her. It was a scene I had long dreaded, and yet, as I reached midlife, knew would come eventually. Seeing Mom approach me as I walked across the polished floor, I thought, "So this is how it has come to be"; at the same time, I told myself, "This is not happening!"

I took my mother in my arms and hugged my sister and brother-in-law. Dale and his wife, Cindy, joined us almost immediately with eighteen-month-old Kaylie. Considering the situation, Mom appeared exceptionally composed, although as she began to explain what had happened I realized that she too was in a state of shock. She told me that Dad had complained of an aching arm that morning before his appointment at the clinic. He had dropped things, a piece of paper here and something else there, before they'd left

Marybeth's house where they had stayed for the weekend. In the waiting-room at the clinic, he had suddenly gripped his arm and gasped. Mom had rushed up to the desk and asked the nurse for help, and they had moved him into a hospital room at once. "There, while a nurse was checking his blood pressure," Mom said to me, her voice breaking for the first time, "Dad's face suddenly puffed up and he lost consciousness." Then she paused as if to catch her breath, and her voice changed to anger. "That nurse should have done something! I told her to do something—and all she said was, 'I'm trying to see what he's doing.'" My mother paused again, her eyes filled with tears, and she added, "The doctor says it was a massive stroke, and he thinks that, based on the x-rays, there's little hope of recovery. Dad's on a respirator, and a brain surgeon is to examine him this evening."

I put my arms around my mother and for a moment stood helplessly, not knowing what to do next. No one else moved either, except Kaylie, who was squirming in her mother's arms. Then, I heard myself say, "I want to see him. I want to be with Dad." Mom led the way.

The room on the fourth floor of the hospital was designed to accommodate two patients. The first bed was empty, however, and Dad's bed was nearest the window, the farthest from the door. With that bed vacant, the room appeared exceptionally large, but in many ways it was a typical hospital room: antiseptically clean, barren of human warmth. The temperature felt chill from the air-conditioning. On one of the walls hung a calendar. I shivered when I saw Dad's inert form and was struck immediately by how serious his condition must be. His head rested on a white pillow, and his body was covered with white sheets and a dark blanket, as if laid out for burial. A blue, plastic tube ran from his nose to the respirator at the side of the bed. From another machine thin, yellow plastic tubes, filled with liquid, were connected to his right arm. I was not affected so much by the sight of these accoutrements of medical wizardry, for I had expected to see them, but by the silence. The only sound in the room was the "whoosh" of the respirator, forcing air in and out of Dad's lungs.

My father seemed asleep. I kissed him on the forehead and took his hand in mine. Then I leaned over to his "good ear" to tell him, "Dad, I'm here. It's Ed. I'm here, Dad." Nothing. "Dad," I repeated, more loudly, "I'm here. It's Eddie. Can you hear me, Dad? Mom and I are here, and the rest of the family is just outside." Then, probably more to reassure myself than him, I said, "You're going to be all right. We love you, and we'll be with you from now on." Still he did not move.

Mom stood next to me weeping. Suddenly she moved to his side, and began to dab at my father's eyes with a tissue. "Don't you see it?" she asked me. "He has tears in his eyes. He had them when Marybeth and Dale came in for the first time this afternoon. And now for you. He knows you're here." I could do nothing but hold his hand and watch my mother wipe the tears away.

When we left his room I asked if a priest had been called. Mom said no, so I went up to the main desk on the floor and requested that if at all possible Dad receive the sacrament of healing. The nurse dialed a number and, after a brief conversation, told us that a Catholic priest would be there in about an hour.

As we waited, a tall medical technician in a white coat went by. Hoping for some reassurance, Mom told him about Dad's tears. The man listened but seemed skeptical. "Any tears," he said, "could only have been a physical reaction of some kind. In his condition your husband really couldn't know that you were there." I wasn't surprised at his opinion but also remembered what I had heard of near-death experiences, how the dying person frequently is aware of everything that is happening around him.

I asked the technician, "When will the brain surgeon be free to examine my father?"

"It'll have to be later this evening," he replied. "The only surgeon on duty is already in the operating room with some-

one else, and another operation has been scheduled immediately after that one." I could tell from his tone of voice that
Dad was not a high priority, that the hospital staff had already
decided there was little hope of his recovery.

When the technician excused himself, there seemed nothing else for us to do but wait, and pray. We huddled together
in the hallway, saying little, until the priest arrived. A man in
his late fifties with gray hair and dark glasses, Father Lewis
was a member of a religious community in Fargo. Among his
other responsibilities, he acted as a chaplain. He shook each
of our hands and then embraced my mother, who hung onto
his every word. I appreciated the man's personal warmth and
his solicitude toward each of us. He invited all of us to gather
around the bed and to hold each other's hands. Then, he
asked us to pray with him the words used for countless other
dying Christians throughout the ages. As he anointed Dad
with holy oil, he encouraged each of us to do the same. We
took turns applying the rich, sweet-smelling oil to Dad's
hands, feet, and forehead. Yes, I thought to myself as I
watched members of my family dab the oil on, this is a saving
ritual that addresses people's fears and attempts to transform
their suffering. This is what pastoral care at its best is meant
to do: comfort the sorrowful, give words to those who cannot
speak, invite people into the sacred mysteries rather than
keeping them at arms' length. Together, we concluded with
the Our Father, begging God as never before to bless our
own father, to forgive us our sins, and deliver us all from evil.
Father Lewis promised to return the following day and
reassured Mom with a parting hug.

Soon after his departure, a physician came in. "Hello, I'm
Dr. Johnson," he introduced himself, and asked, "You are the
Sellner family?" We nodded our heads in unison, feeling both
relieved and apprehensive at what he might tell us. Dr. Johnson
appeared to be in his sixties, with a ruddy complexion, and
white hair. He spoke softly, yet distinctly, conveying the impression that he knew what he was talking about. He informed

us that the surgeon was still in surgery and would not be able to come by that night. "I've seen your husband's x-rays," he said to Mom, reaching out to grasp her hand. "There is not much more that can be done. Tomorrow I'd like to do a brain scan on him, and if there is still no activity you'll have to decide what to do next."

I inquired about our options. He said that there were two: to continue to give Dad food and medication while keeping the respirator going indefinitely, or to stop the respirator and let my father die a natural death. We had already discussed this among ourselves earlier in the evening and had decided that Dad wouldn't want to have a machine continue to pump air into and out of his lungs when there was no hope of recovery. I spoke up for the family, "We want the hospital staff to give its best possible care to Dad, Doctor, but we do not want them to use extraordinary means if it is determined that he is brain-dead."

"I think that's the best decision," he said quietly. Then, he turned to Dad to examine him once more. Just before leaving the room, he briefly opened my father's eyes to look at the pupils. His eyes were blue, the color of mine, the color of my sons'.

Sometime after Dr. Johnson left, our relatives began to arrive. My cousin Doreen, who lives in Fargo, came first, looking for us, wandering down the hall in tears. She was followed by Uncle Bill and Aunt Norma who, though from Kensal, were visiting in Fargo when they heard the news. "We would have come sooner," they said when they found us, "but when we called the clinic to see how your dad was doing, we were told that Ed had checked out. She didn't even bother to inform us that he'd been transferred to St. Luke's! We finally heard from your aunt Mary Lorraine in St. Cloud that he was here."

Shortly afterward Uncle Donnie, looking as if he had aged ten years, and his oldest daughter, Carol, came up to the floor where my family waited. The two of them had been on the road three hours, driving from Kensal to be with us. I soon became aware that this extended family did not come to the hospital out of any sense of obligation. They genuinely loved my parents and were concerned about all of us. Together we struggled to accept Dad's seemingly hopeless condition.

It was well past midnight when people said their good-byes and either returned to hotel rooms or to their homes. Dale and Marybeth left with their families. Mom and I had decided that we would stay at the hospital that night, and I assured my brother and sister that I would call them imme-diately if there was any change. The hospital staff made no objection to Mom's and my remaining in the room with Dad, presuming that he probably would not survive the night. My mother lay down on the unoccupied bed. I covered her with an extra blanket and encouraged her to get some sleep. Then I spread a blanket on the floor, next to Dad's bed, and tried to do so myself. I was too wound up, however, to relax. I knew that this might be our last time together and didn't really care if I had any sleep or not. "Sleep," I thought, "is something I can always have; keeping vigil with my father is more important than anything else."

After Mom had settled down, I got up and moved a chair around to the other side of Dad's bed and firmly grasped his hand in mine. I held on to it as if to life itself. A nurse came in to check the respirator, the tubes, and Dad's physical condi-tion. "How is he?" I asked.

"It won't be long now," she said calmly. "His kidneys already are shutting down." She seemed unperturbed, not lacking in compassion, but resigned to the inevitability that everyone must die.

When she left, except for the wheeze of the respirator and my mother's quiet breathing, an eerie silence filled the room. There was nothing I could do but listen to the awful sound of the machine pumping air into and out of Dad's lungs. As I held his hand I noticed how rough it felt. When I looked down at his gnarled fingers with their thick nails, I saw the calluses from years of hard work.

I held Dad's hand and, as the respirator pumped on, began repeating in a subdued whisper the reassuring words of Julian of Norwich, the great fourteenth-century English mystic whose shrine and cell I had visited a few years before, "All will be well, and all will be well, and all manner of things will be well." It was a prayer to God for Dad and for all of us. Even more, it was an attempt to soothe my father in what I had already concluded might be his transition to another reality. I interrupted this mantra only to rub my father's arm and tell him, "Dad, I don't know if you can hear me or not, but I love you. I will always love you."

Minutes passed. In the silence lines from the poetry of Dylan Thomas, written after his own father's death, suddenly came to me: "Do not go gentle into that good night/Old age should burn and rave at close of day/ Rage, rage against the dying of the light." I felt too numb to rage, too aware of God's presence with us in the room. I did not feel that what was happening here was in any way a dying of light. After all, wasn't this what my spiritual traditions, what my own parents had taught me—that God is light, and that there is life on the other side of death? I recalled the stories that my mother had once read to me. I remembered my father's silent attention when the same stories were read at Sunday Mass—how God in the first moments of creation had said, "Let there be light!", how Moses had come upon the fiery bush at the foot of Mount Horeb and been told that he stood on holy ground, how Jesus' face and body had shone with light on the Mount of the Transfiguration when he conversed with his spiritual ancestors. Images of fire and light are found throughout the scriptures and in the writings of the wisdom figures of Christian spirituality. I knew of the ancient legends of St. Brigit, the Irish spiritual leader, whose life was touched by fire, and whose soul, after she had died, was compared to the sun and to a shining lamp. I thought of how the desert mother Amma Syncletica described God in similar terms, "God is a consuming fire; hence we ought to light the divine fire in ourselves with labor and with tears." I remembered too that John Climacus, the early desert writer at St. Catherine's monastery in the Sinai, had once said, "God is like the outpouring of light, the glimpse of the sun, the changes of the weather."

There in the darkness of that hospital room, with only a faint light filtering through the drawn curtains from the street lamp outside, those stories and sayings inexplicably gave me the power to hope, the ability to see beyond the present uncertainty and to glimpse, at least for the moment, a greater reality. I told myself that there are times one must rage against the dying of the light, but if this is Dad's time to die, who am I to fight it? With that resolution, all I wanted to do was to help Dad through his final passage. I realized that I had my own anointing to do.

I stopped chanting the Julian prayer, let go of my father's hand, and stood over him. Slowly and reverently I began to sign his forehead, arms, hands, and feet again with the sign of the cross. This time, however, I prayed a different refrain, "Go gently, Dad, into light; go gently into light." My actions and prayers were for the man who had given me life, for the parent with whom I had at times fought fiercely, for the close friend whom I had taken too long to recognize.

Only months later did I associate my anointing of Dad with what an Anglican nun, Sister Helen, had shown me three years before, when I was staying in Oxford, England. She had opened an old book and pointed out a paragraph that referred to the *anamchara* or soul friend of the ancient Christian Celts. It described how the soul friend was someone who traditionally ministered to the dying. "In the days of the old Celtic Church," the book read, "the death-croon was chanted over the dying by the *anamchara*, the soul friend." Although I didn't know it at the time I was in that bleak hospital room, anointing my father was part of a wisdom tradition that recognized the value of being with loved ones when they die, and the gift we receive when we are. My prayer earlier that day in the car on the way to Fargo had been answered.

The rest of the night went by quickly. Mom and I had little sleep, taking turns lying on the extra bed and waiting for morning. As the first streaks of dawn colored the sky outside, I tore off the sheet, JULY 22, from the calendar hanging on the wall. In front of my eyes now were the bold, black letters JULY 23. I distinctly recalled biographies of Lutheran theologian Paul Tillich, and of his speaking of his own "dying day." I knew intuitively that this was Dad's.

Like the previous evening, the morning was a blur of fragmented conversations and disjointed memories. I had talked with JoAnne briefly the evening before and now telephoned to tell her that Dad had survived the night. She knew that the medical staff was going to do a brain scan on my father about 10 a.m. "I'll call you as soon as we find out anything," I assured her.

In the meantime Uncle Bill and Aunt Norma returned to the hospital. While Mom stayed with my aunt and my sister Marybeth, who had also come back, Uncle Bill took me down to the coffee shop. My uncle had been a farmer all his life, someone who constantly teased his nieces and nephews while they were growing up—and then *their* children. I had heard years before how he and Uncle Donnie had introduced themselves for the first time to my father. Mom had brought her new beau to meet the relatives on Grandpa's and Grandma's farm outside of Kensal. That night, while Dad had his hands full carrying two pails of milk back from the barn to the house, my two uncles, always mischievous, fired a shotgun into the air as he passed. How they laughed when the milk went flying!

Now, in contrast to earlier times, Uncle Bill seemed to want to have a serious talk with me. We sat down at the counter and ordered coffee and rolls. Then my uncle began to relate his concern about my father. A man of few words, like so many Dakota farmers, he described Dad as "a good friend," and seemed to want to reassure me. "I lost a father too," he told

me, "and I know what you're going through." We discussed
Dad's condition. My uncle agreed with our decision not to use
extraordinary means if there was no hope of Dad's recovery. I
appreciated his kindness at a time when I was feeling unsure
of what to do, and what the morning might bring. Then Uncle
Bill changed the subject to something else he evidently wanted
to discuss. "No matter what happens to your Dad," he said to
me, "you've got to go to Ireland and England as you planned."

"Oh, I just don't know," I replied, surprised that he had
even brought up a topic that was far from my mind. "Everything is so up in the air. If Dad dies, I don't think I could
leave Mom."

"Yes, you can," he responded immediately. "We'll take care
of her." And then he added, "Your dad would want you to go."
We ended our conversation on that note, and my uncle got up
to pay the check.

Two young nurses started the brain scan mid-morning.
They fitted a plastic cap over my father's head and began
monitoring the machine. I stayed for a short time, but they
asked me to leave, telling me that it would be at least an hour
before their work was completed. All of us sat in the lounge
area on the floor where Dad's room was, joining a crowd of
other people who were waiting to hear news of their loved
ones. It all seemed so incongruous—talking to each other
across a room filled with strangers who, preoccupied with
their own anxieties, still seemed to listen in as we discussed
Dad's fate. As I looked around at the strained faces, each of
us immersed in his or her own pain and concern for those
we loved, I had the sense of the fragility of human life, and
of our solidarity.

Finally I could sit no longer. Waiting anxiously for the
medical report, and feeling so powerless, I needed to get
away, to do something, anything. I began to make phone calls
to certain relatives and friends of my parents, telling them of
Dad's stroke, if they hadn't already heard, and asking for
their prayers. Most of my numerous aunts and uncles had

been informed by phone the preceding evening. Uncle Wendy, Dad's oldest brother, was obviously shaken by the news. He wondered aloud why God had allowed this to happen to a younger brother while he remained alive. Next, I got through to Joe, Dad's good friend, the man who had tolerated all those lost gas caps. He and his wife, Irene, had not heard the news. There was a long silence on the other end of the line when I told him. Too upset to talk, Joe handed the phone to Irene, who said they'd be praying for Dad and all of us. She asked that I get back to them as soon as there was something to report.

I returned to the hospital lounge and, along with the others, waited, watching the clock hands make their slow revolution. About noon, Dr. Johnson called us back to the room where Dad lay. Bill and Norma stayed behind, while Marybeth waited for her husband, Jim. I accompanied Mom into the room. "I'm afraid," he said, speaking directly to my mother, "that the brain scan showed no brain activity. There is no hope that your husband will recover." I reached out to Mom as she gasped and seemed about to collapse. "I'm sorry," the doctor told us, "but the stroke was so massive that there was nothing that could be done." Then, as I supported my mother, he turned to me and asked, "What does your family want to do?"

I knew what we had decided. I knew what I had to say. Still, I could hardly breathe, and my mouth went dry. Finally, the words came tumbling out, "We don't want any extraordinary means used to keep his body alive."

"I think that is the best decision," Dr. Johnson replied, sounding almost relieved. Then he added, "We're going to turn off the respirator shortly. Considering that other vital functions have already begun shutting down, I expect that your husband and father will die almost immediately." Then he said to us, "You can leave the room now and wait outside."

I couldn't believe what he had just said. As my mother turned and started for the door, my immediate thought was,

"Oh, God, no! Now is the time that Dad needs us to be with him. Now is not the time for isolation, for a clean medical procedure!" I said aloud to my mother, "No, Mom! We should be with Dad when he dies. I would want him to be with me if I were dying." We stayed, and Dr. Johnson made no objection.

Marybeth and her husband joined us and stood at the foot of the bed. Mom held one of Dad's arms, and I held the other. Dale and Cindy, who had arrived a short time earlier, stayed outside. Dale had told Dad good-bye the night before and felt unable to return to the room where death waited in the shadows. The slow vigil began. It seemed to stretch on forever as the nurse, under Dr. Johnson's watchful eye, slowly shut down the respirator. After approximately ten minutes the machine was totally shut off. Dad took a deep breath when it stopped. His chest tightened and his arms reached upward for a moment, and then he exhaled slowly, almost like a sigh, as if entering into sleep.

I had never been with someone as he died, but I recalled the passing of the early saints, especially St. Cuthbert, a seventh-century holy man, whose death Bede the Venerable described as "stretching out his hands aloft, he sent forth his spirit."

With the last "whoosh" of the machine and Dad's final letting go, silence filled the room, a terrible silence. I could only think one thing: "My God, my father is dead, the man who gave me life, whose name I bear! What am I going to do without him?" Death was no longer a word, an intellectual concept, a distant reality; for me now it was this scene, imprinted on my mind and heart, of one good man dying.

No one moved. Each of us hesitated to turn away from my father's inert body and leave him behind. Finally, I got up from the chair, took my mother's hand, and joined our hands with Marybeth's and Jim's. Father Lewis, who had been with us the previous evening, entered the room with Dale and Cindy and led us in a short prayer for my father. He then took us to a room near the main desk. We were easily led, too numb, too shocked by our sudden loss. While we waited in that small, windowless room, which seemed to suffocate us with its new furniture and antiseptic cleanliness, he went to inform our relatives of Dad's death. We stayed there, looking away when our eyes met. We did not know what to say—nor did we want to say anything at all. We were literally dumbfounded, unable to comprehend the reality that Dad was actually gone.

A short time later I called JoAnne from the same phone that I had used earlier, located in the hall next to the crowded room where strangers waited to hear about their own loved ones. JoAnne accepted the call and listened quietly as my voice broke in telling of Dad's dying. "I'm so sorry," she said softly. I asked her to let me talk to the boys.

"Yes, I'll put them on," she replied, "but I didn't tell either of them how really sick Grandpa was. I didn't want to worry them."

John came on the line crying, just informed that his grandfather was dead. "Daddy, I will miss him so."

"I know, John," I said, as I too began to cry. "He loved you and Daniel very much."

I was at a loss for words, trying to control my tears and to comfort my oldest son at the same time. In the background I heard a loud shriek as JoAnne broke the news to Daniel. Of my two sons, I knew that Daniel was closer to his grandfather, and that he would be the more upset. He came on the line next, sobbing incoherently. "Daniel, you know Grandpa Ed loved you with all his heart and will always be close to you." I let my younger son cry and talk for a while. "We'll get through this together, Dan," I said, before asking to speak to JoAnne once more. "Help your mother get ready to come up here, and I'll see you soon."

JoAnne and I spoke briefly about tentative plans. As I put down the receiver, it came to me how much I would need each of them to get through this hard time.

CHAPTER III

Awakening

If you have a heart, you can be saved.
—Abba Pambo

WE RETURNED THAT TUESDAY AFTERNOON, the day Dad died,
to Kensal, the town where my parents had lived for the past six
years, the site of Dad's and my last battle. Dale and I drove
together. Kensal's main street, with its two bars (one of them
closed), brick post office, grocery store, and lone restaurant
(the town's most popular place), seemed deserted. Once a
thriving community, now, like so many other small towns in
North Dakota, it was rapidly becoming a place inhabited
primarily by ghosts and memories. Numerous houses were
standing empty, many in good condition, and buildings that
had once contained successful businesses were abandoned or
for sale.

I parked the car in the driveway by the house, and then
Dale and I waited for my mother to arrive with Norma. I kept
expecting to see Dad. That was the hardest thing about coming
home—not having him there to welcome us. I remembered the
last time I had been there, in early May, when I had brought
the boys with me. I, of course, had gotten lost on the country
roads, been stopped for speeding by a local sheriff, and had
driven about two hours out of my way by the time I found the
road into Kensal. Dad was there, as usual, at the door. He
listened patiently as I told him angrily about my getting lost,
implying by my tone of voice, I'm sure, that it was somehow

his and Mom's fault for having moved back to that godforsaken town in the first place. Then, along with his sympathy, he offered me, as any good former bartender would, a drink. That was in May, and now in late July, everything had changed.

My mother arrived and led us up the back steps and across the deck. I recalled the good times we had had on that deck during the summers, when Dad would fix steaks on the grill, and we would sit around talking, drinking Manhattans, and watching the boys play. While Mom fumbled with the key, tears came to my eyes as I looked through the glass door at the light and dark spaces of old, familiar rooms. The entire house reminded me of death and loss. Like the town, it was haunted with memories, not only of Dad, but of my grandparents, who had lived there after they had retired from a lifetime of farming. Grandpa John had died in 1972, and Grandma Mary stayed on in the house until she moved to a nearby nursing home. My parents had retired into the same house, so that they could be closer to Grandma Mary and to my mother's siblings. I had brought my sons up to see their grandparents before and after Grandma Mary's death in 1986. They had sat at the same place for breakfast where I had sat when I was a child, watching Grandpa John peel an orange, and, most amazingly, eat not only the orange but the peels! Daniel had tossed and turned in his sleep in the same bed and in the same room where I had, years before, slept with my grandfather. John had run through the garden where my grandmother had once planted vegetables and waited, not always patiently, for their maturation. The preceding Thanksgiving our family had gathered in the same living room where my cousins and I as teen-agers had watched the television screen following John Kennedy's assassination.

Now, standing in the family room my uncle Bill had added on when my parents had moved in, I felt as if the entire house reverberated with the absence of those whom I loved deeply. I missed my father especially. "God," I said to Mom and Dale, "it seems so empty without him!"

The three of us walked around like zombies. Most of all, we tried getting used to the idea that Dad was not going to join us. Mom decided to make coffee, and, as the three of us sat at the kitchen table, we began making suggestions about various things that had to be done for the wake and funeral. Within minutes, however, the phone rang, and didn't stop the rest of the afternoon as word spread that we were back. As is typical of life—and death—in a small town, concerned neighbors began to drop by that day and the next with food and a few kind words to sustain the family. In between greeting visitors and answering the phone, I decided to go for a walk. I wanted to get some needed exercise, I told myself, as well as to try to clear my head. Really, I just wanted to get away, to escape for a while the constant talk of death.

I walked across the front yard and came to a standstill under the elms planted by Grandpa John. There, still visible in the grass, were the rut marks where Dad had told me to park the car on my last visit in early May. I stared down at them, remembering. The visit had been pleasant—except for the six to eight inches of snow that had fallen throughout our second day there. Ah, good old Kensal weather, I thought to myself. Even in May there's ice and snow!

During that visit my parents, John, Daniel, and I had decided to drive to Jamestown, a town about twenty-five minutes away, on Saturday afternoon. In order to use my parents' Oldsmobile, which had more room than my Toyota, Dad told me to park my car on the snow-covered grass under the trees. I had hesitated, and told him, "I don't think so, Dad. The ground seems awfully soft there, and I may get stuck."

"Go ahead," he said unfazed. "It won't be a problem." I still had my doubts but followed his directions.

The next day I packed the suitcases, put them in the trunk, and started the car. Dad and Mom were beside the car, waiting to tell us good-bye. The only sound, however, was that of my spinning tires—and of my cursing. We weren't going anywhere, except deeper into the mud and slush. I alternately put the car forward and in reverse. Then I noticed the look on Dad's face change from surprise to hostility to outrage. I immediately recognized that look, that angry spark in his eyes. I remembered it well from my youth, adolescence, and adulthood.

"What are you doing to my lawn?" he yelled.

The battle was once again joined, and I angrily replied, "Why did you tell me to park here, anyway? I told you the ground was too soft!"

We glared at each other, and yelled, and the mud, along with our words, flew madly. Once again, my mother tried to intercept and intercede, but neither of us listened.

Then, suddenly, I stopped. I realized that it just wasn't worth it anymore. At the same moment Dad recognized this too. Our years of fighting weren't really all that important now; neither of us had to win this battle or continue the war between us. The air cleared, and the fury of years of disagreements and the need to prove through angry confrontation our worth to each other was gone, finally spent. I could almost hear, as I took my foot off the accelerator, the laying down of arms.

Behind his angry words, I also heard—as I became able to listen—not only his concern for the green grass that he had nurtured out of a section of the yard that once had nothing but dust, but also his hurt that I was blaming him again, calling him, again, the stupid one.

I stopped my impatient running of the engine, the lurching back and forth between forward and reverse, and listened as he suggested that we get my cousin to pull me out with his pickup truck. Once my car was free, I got out to thank my cousin Cletus for his help and to apologize to my father for the harm done to the yard. Dad nodded his acceptance and said, "You'd better get new tires; it's obvious they're worn." He made the suggestion without rancor and, pointing to the boys, added, "I'd be worried about their safety." I nodded, and the three of us kissed Mom and Dad good-bye. We drove off with both my parents' tired smiles visible in the rearview mirror, waving at us as we turned the corner.

Driving back to St. Paul that May, I felt as if the cycle had at last been broken: the old mutually-destructive pattern of hurts, recriminations, resentments, and further distancing that we had fallen into so frequently. Old tensions over authority, identity, and self-worth for each of us seemed finally to have been laid to rest. Somehow I no longer felt I had to prove myself to him. Perhaps he felt the same.

During the next three months the ruts and my tires became a source of humorous phone conversation. Dad would ask, "Did you get new tires?"

I would respond, "Did you get the grass re-sodded?"

Standing there now, staring down at the still visible tire marks, I saw that he had not bothered to fill in the ruts with grass. "Maybe he didn't have time," I said to myself. "Or maybe he just decided that the marks didn't matter." I was happy, though, that I had listened to him about the tires. I had had them replaced a week before Dale's phone call. Stooping down and tracing the tracks with my fingers, I thought of how much had happened in the twenty-four hours since I had picked up the receiver in St. Paul.

I slept soundly that night, physically and emotionally exhausted. I awoke only once, when I heard a cough that I thought was Dad's. At about the same time a train whistle blew, its long, mournful sound echoing my sadness.

The following morning I opened my eyes with a jolt, bewildered, wondering where I was. Then the horrible realization hit like a sledgehammer. My father was dead! Before, I had been too shocked to experience the awful pain of loss. Now it felt as if I had been sliced open and that a knife with jagged edges was slashing even deeper cuts. As I left the bedroom, I saw my mother leaning over the bathtub, sobbing as she rinsed her hair, her tears mingling with the rushing water.

Dale joined us for breakfast. My brother was late to rise and had few words to say, caught up in his own form of grieving. Tall, muscular, a born athlete, he silently finished his breakfast and said that he was going over to our cousin Cletus's house. He too seemed uncomfortable with the never-ending talk of death. I told him that I'd come over and get him when we were ready to drive to Jamestown to make the funeral arrangements. As he left, I thought of how much like Dad he was, how difficult it was to communicate with him. Of course my being gone all those years when I was in the seminary hadn't helped our relationship. Nor did the memory of Dad's pride the year Dale's basketball team won the state tournament. It was Dale's basket in the last minute that had broken a tied game. I had genuinely shared my father's pride. There was no doubt, either, that I loved my younger brother. But deep down, the memory of his winning basket had grated, as had the look of joy that spread across my father's face.

With Dale gone, I helped my mother with the dishes. The phone began to ring once more, and I listened again to Mom repeat the story of Dad's stroke and its aftermath. She seemed to find greater solace each time she told the story. Finally, in mid-morning, Mom, Dale, and I drove to Jamestown. Dan Lisko, the funeral director who had arranged Grandma Mary's funeral five years earlier, met us in his office on the first floor. A slightly balding man in his early forties, with two children of his own, Mr. Lisko greeted us warmly and explained what decisions had to be made about Dad's wake, funeral, and burial. He gave enough information without pressuring us. My mother showed him the clothes that she had chosen for Dad: gray pants, a light shirt, peach-colored tie, and a rose-colored sportcoat that, she said, "he always was so proud of." "I know some will think he should be in a suit," she told us, "but that was his favorite outfit."

Mr. Lisko led us to the basement where a large variety of coffins were on display. I hadn't realized how many types of coffins there were—nor all the interiors and colors from which one could choose! We picked out a simple bronze coffin. Then we returned to the office and were shown even more varieties of memorial cards. Dale and I, of course, disagreed on the card's design, but Mom broke the logjam, deciding on a plain white card with a simple gold cross on the front. We agreed on plans for a wake at the Lisko Funeral Chapel the next afternoon, a prayer service in Kensal that night, and the funeral the following morning.

When we returned to Kensal in mid-afternoon, I drove out alone to the Roman Catholic cemetery. Here my maternal grandparents were buried, and here my father's body was soon to lie. My parents, with Uncle Bill and Aunt Norma, had already chosen adjoining lots, but no decision had been made where either couple would finally rest. The cemetery was just a couple of minutes drive from Kensal, less than ten minutes on foot. The sun had disappeared behind a blanket of dark, gray clouds spread across the vast Dakota sky. "The wide, open spaces of the prairie," I said to myself as I got out of the car and noticed how quiet it was. Not even a bird singing. On all sides were black, red, and brown granite tombstones, carved with the names of pioneers. Twelve stately evergreens dotted the site, and peony bushes, covered now with only dark, green leaves, were planted near some of the graves. Not far from a storage shed and a rusting well-pump was the figure of the crucified Jesus, painted white, hanging on a large black wooden cross. It stood in the center of this cleared oasis, surrounded by miles of wind-tossed wheat and corn.

I stopped a moment for a prayer at my grandparents' grave, which was overshadowed by the long branches of one of the evergreens. Grandpa John and Grandma Mary were ancestors with whom I felt spiritually and emotionally connected, and upon whose gravesite I had, the previous summer, put a lawn chair and spent the afternoon. I was following the custom of desert Christians and my own early Celtic ancestors, who believed that people need to communicate with the dead and that praying at their tombs can be especially efficacious. Writing in my journal, while sitting at their graves, I had carried on a conversation with them, listening to what, in prayer, they might teach me. A chicken-hawk hovered in the air above. I could almost hear my grandparents speak.

Earlier on the day of that extended cemetery visit, I had been reading a novel by Reynolds Price, who said that "the dead have lives of their own." I agreed with him, but I also believed that the dead are not totally cut off from *our* lives. "There is the very vivid sense that you are close by," I told my grandparents, speaking directly to them, "and that when we call upon you, you will be there." I told them again how much I loved and missed them. I told them of my worries, of my concerns about teaching, of my hopes that I would become a more loving person to my parents, wife, sons, and friends. In the quiet air I had heard my grandparents respond. My Grandpa John replied that he had always loved me, his second oldest grandchild. He said that I didn't have to worry so much about where my life was leading me. "Remember how you used to worry when you were a kid, and I'd disappear into the rows of corn, leaving you in the pickup, wondering where I'd gone? Well, didn't I always return?" he had asked. "Don't worry, then; worrying's only a waste of time."

My Grandma Mary also had something to say. She had reassured me that same afternoon, "I'll always be there for you, Eddie. After all, wasn't I there when you were just a child staying on the farm? Remember your uncles, Bill and Donnie, and how they would squirt you with milk when you got too close to them in the barn as they were milking cows? I was there to protect you, then. Nothing has changed." Grandma Mary had also reminded me that afternoon of the need for prayer. "Even when I got so old that there was little I could do physically anymore, remember, Ed, how I kept on praying—for my loved ones, for you?"

I trusted my grandparents implicitly. Death had not interrupted my relationship with them. Now, alone with them in the cemetery once again, I asked them, "Help me, Grandpa and Grandma, choose a proper site for Dad's body, and welcome him into your own company."

As I lifted my eyes from their graves, I saw immediately the ground in which my father's body would lie. It was just across the small gravel road that divided the cemetery in half. Of the two lots already chosen by my parents and aunt and uncle for their resting places, I knew that the site nearest the road was the most appropriate place for Dad. Hadn't he been, all his life, a bartender, a tavern owner, constantly welcoming people? Wouldn't he want to have his grave closest to where people walked or drove? I walked across the brown grass, parched by the heat of the sun, and stood, looking down at where we would carry my father's body in less than two days. "Dad," I said aloud in the silence of the graves, "this is where you will rest from your labors." There was no sound but a breeze rustling the leaves and pine cones and stirring slightly the golden wheat in the nearby fields.

The rest of the afternoon and evening we continued to make decisions about the wake, prayer service, and funeral. Marybeth had driven into Kensal while the three of us had been in Jamestown. When she met us at the door, I saw how much Dad's death had affected her. The youngest child, she had been the most reticent at sharing her views and feelings, at least with her two older brothers. Always somewhat reserved, she now seemed even more withdrawn, crushed by the death of her father. She sat quietly in the living room as we discussed details and, every once in awhile, offered her suggestions. For pallbearers, we decided to ask two of my father's closest friends: Wally, one of the farmers from Edgeley with whom Dad and Mom had frequently fished when they retired, and Joe, my former boss at the service station. Besides them, I called my father's three brothers and three brothers-in-law to make sure that they could serve in that capacity. We had earlier asked my cousin Kathy, the church organist, to play for the prayer service and the funeral. She stopped by before supper to help us pick out the hymns. We chose a combination of traditional and contemporary songs, including "How Great Thou Art," "On Eagles' Wings," and the "Prayer of St. Francis." The latter hymn was a favorite of Dad's. Like the medieval saint, my father had loved and cared for birds since his retirement, hanging numerous feeders around the outside of the house in Kensal. On my visits home, I was amazed that he could identify by name the large number of birds that came for their daily feed. He and Mom had given us a number of bird feeders over the years, which JoAnne and I had received politely, with little enthusiasm. We believed that we already had enough people and projects to care for—without adding birds to the list. Now, in planning the funeral, it seemed only right to include the St. Francis song.

After supper Mom, Marybeth, Dale, and I put together a collage of photos on a small bulletin board. Each of the pictures was familiar to us, but now, put together for the first time, they told the story of Dad's life, showing us what we had had only intimations of before. They also expressed what he meant to us as individuals. "Put this one in," Dale had said. So we added a picture of Dad standing proudly beside a fighter plane that he had flown in World War II. The plane had large numerals, 42, painted on its tail.

"This has to be included," Marybeth suggested quietly. "It's the picture of Dad and Mom in the new bar." There they stood at the grand opening in Wyndmere, surrounded by plants and flowers from well-wishers. Both of them looked so young and happy, so excited about their new venture among new friends.

My mother picked out one of Dad at a lake, holding up a string of six large Northerns. "Now, did he catch all those himself?" she laughed. She couldn't honestly remember, but the number and size of the fish led us to suspect that he probably had had some help. My father always enjoyed those fishing trips as a chance to relax and put aside his worries.

We chose at least ten more of Dad with his brothers, mother, children, grandchildren, in-laws, friends. I selected two of Dad with my sons. In the first he is holding John, who has long baby curls, and standing outside our house on Griggs Avenue in St. Paul. In the second picture Daniel, wearing a Twins baseball cap, is in Dad's arms in the kitchen

of our new house on Princeton. Both sons are smiling
happily, as is Dad, obviously content at being a grandfather.
To these two pictures my brother added one of Dad with his
daughter, Kaylie. Dad has his head thrown back in laughter,
and she is smiling back at him. For all of us, those were the
hardest to look at, the ones of Dad with his three
grandchildren.

As we finished our work on the collage, Father Leo Kuhn
dropped by to discuss the plans for the prayer service and
funeral Mass. Father Kuhn was pastor in Carrington, but, due
to the priest shortage, had also been assigned to the parish in
Kensal. He was the same priest who had inspired me in Edgeley
to join the seminary; he had maintained his ties with our family
for over thirty years. One of my first mentors, I considered him
a good friend and highly appreciated that he would be the
celebrant. Leo hugged each of us and expressed his sympathy.
Mom especially was moved by his compassion. Sometime
during our conversation, he asked me if I wanted to give a short
reflection at the end of the liturgy for the family. I had been
expecting that he would ask me, but I hesitated now, preferring
to stay in the pew. "I just don't know, Leo," I told him. "I don't
know if I would be able to get through it without breaking
down." He respected my wishes and advised me to think about
it some more before deciding. When he left, we retired for the
night, aware that we needed all the strength we could muster
for the following day.

I awoke suddenly in the middle of the night, sitting bolt
upright in bed. Wide awake, the first words from my mouth
were, "By God, you did it. You did it, Dad! You accomplished
what I only hope I can by the time I die!" I turned on the light,
and rummaged around for a pen and paper, intent now on
giving the talk at my father's funeral. I had something to say
that no one else there could. Somewhere between falling
asleep and awakening with a start, I had become aware that I
had never really seen my father as he was. I had had intimations
of this earlier, almost three years before, when I had first

realized how judgmental I'd been toward Dad for much of my adult life. But now it was even clearer. Dad's death had shed new light on old "tapes" that repeatedly played back the same distorted tunes. Those memories and feelings from fights and disagreements when I was growing up had kept me from fully appreciating him. My leaving home so young probably hadn't helped erase those impressions! They had hindered me from seeing how much Dad had changed over the years, and how much I had missed.

I had always remembered him as a "stubborn German," as my mother once called him, overly defensive at times and prone to sitting on his anger until it erupted unpredictably. But now, in the night's stillness, I saw his anger as a sign of his convictions and of his concern for me. Yes, he overreacted at times, but he evidently felt that he sometimes had to do so to get my attention. Even most recently, when he had scolded me for working too hard, I now realized, he had been speaking out of his care for me. I had said nothing at the time. Here was the man who had spent his lifetime overworking, and he was telling me to stop!

No doubt about it, Dad overworked. He complained constantly of his long hours and of seeing "the same old faces" day after day and night after night. As an adolescent I didn't know how to respond to his complaints, and so I said little, probably leaving him with the impression that I didn't care. On another level, I think I resented his tiredness and what I perceived as his lack of interest in me. He would come home from work and fall asleep in front of the television set, and yet he always seemed to be available for someone else—a customer or stranger. Almost every Christmas Eve my brother, sister, mother, and I would wait for him to return from work so we could finally open our gifts. "I just couldn't get rid of the customers," he'd say. We didn't understand, nor did we accept that excuse from him.

Now I recognized that there were reasons for his overwork. If Dad had trouble setting limits to it, so did all those who, like him, had faced the Great Depression and survived. They knew the nagging fear of not making ends meet, and they fought it by working constantly. They also did it because they were genuinely concerned about their families. If Dad—and Mom—had not worked so hard, my sister, brother, and I wouldn't have had the opportunities we later did. Dad worked because he cared about us. And he continued to do so even after he retired. I remembered, in particular, all the times he had washed my car when I visited him and Mom. Even when he came to visit us in St. Paul, he'd get the hose going and wash and wax. In the fall he'd help me rake the thousands of leaves that fell into our yard and wash the storm windows for the coming winter. "Work goes faster," he told me, "when we do it together." In the spring we would take them down and replace them with the screens. One summer he and Mom even volunteered to paint our house so that JoAnne and I could save money to pay some of our other bills. And they did it!

Dad had consistently been a kind and generous human being—up to the last day we spent together when he had offered to buy me a drink at the park and to pay for my boys' rides. He was a hospitable man—not only to me, but to all sorts of people over a lifetime. If, when I was young, he brought home and fed people, some of whom I had considered despicable, maybe it was because he knew what it was to be without work. Maybe he realized how much they would appreciate a homecooked meal. Even in Kensal, as I had learned the past days, Dad had touched a lot of people's lives—from the young girl across the street who said he always gave her money for an ice cream cone to the elderly in the nursing home who said they'd miss his delivery of "Meals on Wheels." My cousin Cletus had told me the day before, "Your dad was like a second father to me."

As I sat on the side of my bed writing on a yellow pad, I remembered Dad's difficulty expressing feelings other than anger. I had tried on a number of occasions to get him to talk about himself, and about our relationship, but to little avail. Before I married JoAnne I had sent him a letter in which I discussed my experiences of growing up: both the happy and painful times. I had also expressed my love for him. He didn't mention the letter until I asked him outright months later. All he said then was, "I didn't think it was that bad." I had not pursued the topic, for he had seemed embarrassed and hurt by my references to the past. I think I too was probably afraid at what he might tell me.

But, I now recalled, he *had* tried at different times to talk with me. He *had* made attempts at giving me advice. There was the conversation with him in the bar before I left for the seminary. There was the time at JoAnne's grandmother's lake home when he suggested that I find ways to relax. "You've got to slow down a bit. Maybe take up golf." He seemed nervous when he suggested this, hesitant, fearful at how I might react. Afraid of me? That thought hadn't crossed my mind.

Sometimes he did speak up, assertively. When I had complained, for example, about what I considered his push to start painting the house so early on a Saturday morning, he simply said, "If you didn't want me to start painting the house at 8 a.m., all you had to do was tell me." Or the time when I was outraged at a pastor whose homilies demeaned the laity and offered little in the way of spiritual sustenance. I had argued vehemently with my mother about him. She thought that I should just endure the situation. It was Dad who had said, "Well, if you can't pray there, then join another parish where you can."

My father may have had trouble talking about his own feelings, but so did his entire generation of males, who had never learned a vocabulary for naming their affective side, let alone been encouraged to acknowledge it. He had not had any clinical training, studied psychology, or received years of spiritual direction—as I had. If Dad didn't know how to talk about our relationship, it wasn't all his fault. And if my father came home tired, as he did when I was young, and failed to talk with me, maybe, just maybe, it was because I always had my head buried in a book.

Books—that is where I found my first heroes. That's where I spent so much of my time. Those whom I considered to be my mentors when I was growing up, Thomas Merton, Robert Kennedy, Paul Tillich, C. S. Lewis, and Carl Jung were figures larger than life. What I knew about them came from their own writings or from admiring biographers. Even the saints whom I had been studying, both those from the desert and from Celtic lands, were frequently portrayed by their hagiographers as having been born into a state of holiness rather than to have struggled for it one day at a time. My father always suffered by comparison.

I thought of what I had been teaching students for years, from a variety of psychological and spiritual traditions, about what constitutes authentic spirituality. Carl Jung uses psychological language to explain his understanding. He speaks of "individuation," a process especially critical at mid-life, when we begin to live less centered in the ego and more centered in the soul. He compares it to an alchemical process that necessarily involves being "near the fire," a willingness to endure—not run away from—suffering so that transformation can occur. People who are committed to individuation manifest, he says, certain qualities; honesty, integrity, dedication to getting at the truth of their lives. Besides faith, hope, and love, Christianity associates holiness with these same qualities. Perfection is not one of them. Our spiritual traditions never have said that true holiness is the eradication of all temptations or even that we never fail. Rather, true holiness is centering our lives in God, serving others as best we can, and being committed, with God's help, to the struggle. The desert Christians, in particular, said that "the soul is matured only in battles." They told the story of an elder who prayed, when temptations came, not that the struggle be taken from him, but only, "Lord, give me strength to get through the fight."

Now I realized that of all those saintly heroes about whom I had written and taught, of all those heroes who had lived a thousand years ago or more, it was Dad, right under my nose, who had integrated into his own life those qualities that my Christian faith holds dear. My father, with his hospitality, compassion, and willingness to forgive, was far more individuated than I had ever given him credit for. God knows he struggled—long nights and days in the bar—with conflicts and problems of which I had no inkling.

This is what evidently had come to me earlier in my dreams that night when I had awakened with such a start. Somewhere between my head hitting the pillow and opening my eyes, I recognized my blindness. I understood that there were more factors affecting Dad's and my relationship than I had originally imagined, that what I had at one time identified as his weaknesses were, in fact, his strengths. Of course Dad made mistakes raising his children—everyone does. But, if he didn't express himself well verbally, that was not to say he didn't love us. He had consistently proven his love not so much by words, but by deeds, and, yes, I thought, as I continued to write, by his tears.

An afternoon came to mind when I was leaving Wyndmere to return to the seminary. The sun was shining brightly, but I felt extremely tense. I was telling both of my parents good-bye. Again. We were standing out by the old garage, near the road that led up to my dad's bar on the corner of Mainstreet. As I kissed my mother and turned to give Dad a hug, I noticed that his eyes were filled with tears, and that he was trying to hold them back. He seemed embarrassed and turned away. Mom spoke for him, as usual. "Your dad," she said, "is going to miss you too." I didn't know what to say to him, but I hugged him and let him cry. I was embarrassed by *his* emotions! I was afraid that *I* might cry!

As I sat there writing on the edge of the bed the night before his wake, that memory of saying farewell to him reminded me of the scene in the hospital room where Dad

lay dying and Mom had pointed out his tears. I had not really
wanted to see them. They reminded me too much of vul-
nerability. I had not thought of them as signs of love.

I set aside my pen and pad and turned out the light. In
the darkness I remembered my last conversation with Dad,
the weekend following his surprise birthday party. He and
Mom had returned to Marybeth's house near Fargo, and I
had called there to see if their trip back had gone all right.
I spoke with Mom first, as was customary, and then she said
to me, "Do you want to talk to Dad?" I had said, "Yes, put
him on." We had talked briefly about his birthday party and
whether he had gotten any fish at the lake on his way home.
As we were closing, I said to him, "Dad, I love you." Without
a moment's hesitation, he had said with emotion in his voice,
"I love you too." Those four words seemed to have taken him
a lifetime to say. They had come to his lips so readily, perhaps
because of the birthday party and the look we had exchanged
near the lilac bushes when he had cried—and I had not
allowed myself to do the same. Perhaps they came because
he finally believed that I really did love him, despite what I
had once told him years before, "I wish you weren't my
father."

Now, as I tried to sleep once more in the house that seemed
so lonesome without him, I felt a tremendous sense of emptiness, a void in my life that could never be filled, a horrible
feeling of being orphaned. At the same time, I felt strangely
exhilarated at what the darkness had revealed. I thanked God
for having given me such a father, and that his last words to
me were those of love.

Psychologists warn how, after someone dies, we tend to
idealize the dead by exaggerating the person's virtues and
minimizing his or her limitations. I'm not so sure that's what
actually occurs. It may be, rather, that we at last see the dead
as they were—people like us, struggling to survive the vicissitudes of life, making mistakes, trying to learn from them,
doing the best they can. Sometimes, it seems, only death

helps us to see those whom we love as God sees them—in their entirety, not distorted by our own unrealistic expectations, hurt feelings, or wounded memories.

CHAPTER IV

No Regrets

> A certain brother came to Abba Poemen and
> said: "What ought I to do, Father? I am in great
> sadness." The elder said to him: "Never despise
> anything, never condemn anybody, never speak
> evil of anyone, and the Lord will give you peace."

THE NEXT MORNING I TOLD MY MOTHER of my decision to
speak for the family at Dad's funeral. She seemed happy and
relieved. "So, what do you remember most about Dad?" I asked
her, in hopes of including her recollections in my remarks. It
was obviously a difficult question for her. She turned her eyes
from me and stared into space, thinking back over the life that
they had shared for more than fifty years, from the time they
had first met until his death.

"What stands out most about your father," she said finally,
"was his kindness and generosity. Why, the first year we were
going together, I remember him returning to Springfield to
work in the mills for the summer when his own father was ill.
He'd send his paychecks to his mother to help them get
through that hard time." She paused again, and then continued, "He was always doing something for someone—the
years in the bar, listening to drunks till all hours of the night,
even bringing some of them home for supper to help sober
them up if they'd had too much to drink."

"I remember some of those episodes," I told her. "I
couldn't understand why Dad was so nice to some of the

strangest people. Remember that man people called Smut?
Dad gave him a job painting the house."

"How could I forget?" my mother replied. "He took
forever."

"Yes, and I don't think he ever took a bath," I said. "And
what about Dorothy, who was always drunk? I think Dad was
her main support, trying to get her off the sauce. But she didn't
seem to be able to quit, and everybody ridiculed her."

"Everybody but your father."

"Then there was that farmer who always needed to talk to
Dad after everyone else had left. Dad wanted to close up the
bar, he told me, and this man insisted on telling Dad, night
after night, his woes."

"Well," Mom responded, "your dad didn't know how to
say no. But the farmer did eventually manage to straighten
out." A smile crossed her face as she recalled something else
about my father. "Every night after we retired and moved to
Kensal," she said, "your dad came and kissed me before I went
to bed." Then she paused and began to cry. "He was such a
night owl, but I probably should have stayed up with him. What
am I going to do without him?"

I was concerned about my mother that Thursday morning.
I also was anxious about my wife and sons who, with JoAnne's
parents, were preparing to leave for the wake at Jamestown.
JoAnne had told me on the phone that she would have liked
to have come up sooner, but it was a matter of making
arrangements for her to be off from work and getting things
organized with her parents and the boys. I knew that she could
handle the trip up and would get through this time of grief
well. A highly sensitive, sensible, and intuitive woman, she had
inner resources that constantly amazed me. Our relationship
had deepened over the years as we endured the stress of two
full-time jobs and, through forgiveness and acceptance, the
conflicts brought on by the interplay of two distinct personalities. Twelve years together had taught us that marriage
is not the obliteration of differences but living more creatively

with them. A saying from the Irish poet, William Butler Yeats, which I had framed for JoAnne on her fortieth birthday, expressed my appreciation of that awareness and my hope of our growing old together:

> How many loved your moments of glad grace,
> And loved your beauty with love false or true,
> But one man loved the pilgrim soul in you,
> And loved the sorrows of your changing face.

I knew JoAnne was very fond of my parents, as I was of hers; I knew that my father's dying would be a personal loss for her too. I wanted to be with her, and also to be attentive to our sons.

I was aware from books that I had read on grief that younger people are frequently overlooked at times of bereavement. As Mom, Dale, Marybeth, and I left for the funeral home where the visitation was to begin, I decided that as a parent I needed to somehow invite my two sons into the mystery of their grandfather's death without forcing it upon them. I wanted to talk with them, show them Dad in his coffin, let them see death without making them afraid. I also wanted to let them see that it's good for both adults and children to cry when someone they love dies, and that such tears are a normal part of life. I was intent upon not shunting them aside, disregarding their feelings of loss as I tried to deal with my own. Most of all, I wanted to help them see, not only at this time of sudden loss, but throughout life, that God is found at the center of human experiences.

We arrived at the funeral home about 10 a.m. Dan Lisko had everything ready. My father's casket was open, with large and small bouquets of flowers on either side. A kneeler was placed in front of the coffin for people to view the body and to pray. The collage of pictures from Dad's life was set to one side. Dale, Marybeth, and I were silent, caught up in our grief, unable to comprehend how all of this could have happened so suddenly. Dale and Cindy knelt together for a short time, and then Marybeth and Jim. Mom and I went next, and, while there, my mother patted Dad's hands and cried softly.

I looked down at my father's body in the coffin. I stared at his face and hands. His gray hair was neatly combed, and he looked quite natural, almost as if he were asleep. And yet there was something strangely unfamiliar about him: the waxen face, powdered and rouged, the bent fingers with the rosary protruding between them. "It's Dad," I thought to myself, "but it's not him at all!" The man whom I knew and loved and with whom I had spent the night in the hospital room was *not* there.

For the next six hours we greeted relatives and friends as they arrived. Many had been with Dad at our surprise birthday party in what now seemed like years before. I shook their hands or hugged them and listened as they took their turns expressing their grief and love. It seemed so ironic that this sad family reunion followed so closely the happy one just a week ago. In the midst of watching people as they entered and greeting each of them, I grew increasingly apprehensive, wondering what was keeping JoAnne and the boys. Finally they arrived, looking tired and hot from the long trip in the summer heat. I crossed the room immediately and gave JoAnne a kiss, and each of her parents, Mel and Rita, a hug. John kissed me shyly on the cheek, and I hugged him and Daniel tightly. Daniel, who is more apt to speak his mind than John, angrily expressed his grief and his own understanding of his grandfather's death. "If God took Grandpa, I can forgive him," he told me, "but if the devil took him, the devil's a jerk!"

I led all of them over to the coffin. While they knelt in prayer, the bouquet from the three grandchildren arrived. It was a special arrangement, consisting of three red roses with the phrase, "Grandpa, we love you" printed on a blue ribbon, with the names of John, Daniel, and Kaylie underneath. I had noticed earlier, when Dale and Cindy had arrived with Kaylie, that she didn't know what to do with her grandpa in the coffin. She recognized him but didn't understand why he stayed where he was; she kept motioning for him to get up.

We had a short prayer service later in the afternoon. Then Dad's coffin was placed in the hearse. I helped Mr. Lisko put the flowers, memorial cards, and the collage of pictures in beside it. Both of my sons wanted to ride with the undertaker, evidently seeing a ride in a hearse as a great adventure. I told them, "Yes, you can ride with Mr. Lisko, but behave yourselves." The rest of us followed. I drove Mom and Marybeth in my parents' white Oldsmobile—the one I had always hated to drive because of its size. JoAnne followed in her car with her parents. The others had already gone ahead of us to eat supper and prepare for the prayer service that evening.

There were only a few cars on the road between Jamestown and Kensal. We had little to say to each other as we passed fields of wheat and corn. This was farm country, and men and women were going about their work in the farmyards and on tractors in the fields. The most beautiful sight was the thousands of bright, yellow sunflowers basking in the heat. At one point I noticed the hearse ahead of us swerve toward the ditch unexpectedly and then suddenly return to its proper lane.

"I see Daniel has convinced Mr. Lisko that he can drive," I said dryly, and both Mom and Marybeth smiled.

Daniel confirmed my suspicions when he jumped out, once we had arrived in Kensal, and happily told me, "Dan Lisko let me drive!" John, his older brother, nodded his head and raised his eyes to the heavens.

That evening the church in Kensal was crowded with relatives and friends for the prayer service. It was unbearably hot inside the modern circular structure, which had replaced the old white clapboard church in which my grandparents had once worshipped. The new church with its brick exterior had soaked up the heat of the sun throughout the day, and flies buzzed from one mourner to another. On the white walls, plainly visible, were the old stations of the cross from the original church. They had been tastefully repainted by the parish women when the priest who had had them all whitewashed left. I could see by the prominent place of the statue of Mary near the altar that some of the priest's other "reforms" after Vatican II had also failed to take hold. It wasn't that the parishioners didn't welcome the changes of Vatican II. They were just adverse to throwing all those familiar objects out that they identified with their spiritual life. It had been my grandmother who had rescued the statue of Mary from the church basement when my grandfather had reported that he'd found her abandoned with the other statues. Grandpa John swore that he had found the statue with tears in her eyes, and that he had taken out his handkerchief and wiped them away.

Besides that rescued statue, I could see other religious items in the church identified with my grandparents. The gold tabernacle on the altar against the wall had been given to the parish in memory of my grandfather, and on the eucharistic altar were two gold candlesticks donated in memory of Grandma Mary. "My grandparents clearly made their mark," I thought as I glanced around the interior of the church, "but even more than this physical evidence was the gift of faith that they passed on to each of us." I remembered those Sunday mornings in the old clapboard church when my grandparents and all of my relatives, including my cousins and I, sat together in the pews near the front. We knew who we were then. From the oldest to the youngest, we knew our identity. We were a family, a clan whose lineage flowed from the love of John and Mary.

After the opening hymn at the prayer service, Father Kuhn welcomed everyone and then led us all in prayer. In between scripture readings, my mother got up and read a poem from a tea-towel that JoAnne and I had brought Dad from Ireland nine years before. He was fond of it, and, after he had retired to Kensal had put it on the wall in the basement behind his bar. On this colorful towel was the picture of a bartender surrounded by bottles of whiskey and kegs of Guinness pouring a beer. The words of the poem printed below the picture captured the vocation of being a bartender—whether in the Ireland or North Dakota:

> He deserves a hero's medal
> for the many lives he saved.

And upon the Roll of Honor,
    his name should be engraved.
He deserves a lot of credit
    for the way he stands the strain.
For the yarns he has to swallow
    would drive most of us insane.
He must pay the highest licence,
    he must pay the highest rent.
He must battle with his bank
    and pay their ten percent.
And when it comes to paying bills,
    he's always on the spot.
He pays for what he sells,
    whether you pay him or not.
And when you walk into his bar,
    he'll greet you with a smile.
Be you a workman dressed in overalls
    or a banker dressed in style.
If you're Irish, English, Scots, or Welsh,
    it doesn't matter what.
He'll treat you like a gentleman,
    unless you prove you're not.
Yet the clergy in the pulpit
    and the preacher in the hall
Will assure him that the churches
    are against him one and all.
But when the churches plan to hold
    a ballot or bazaar,
They start by selling tickets
    to the man behind the bar.
When he retires, a job well done,
    to await six feet of soil,
Discards his coat and apron,
    no more on earth to toil,
As St. Peter sees him coming,
    he will leave those gates ajar.
For he knows he had his hell on earth,
    the man behind the bar.

As my mother read this poem, I noticed smiles on many faces in the congregation as people recognized in its humor the truth of my father's life and ministry.

When the prayer service was over, Dan Lisko asked me if I wanted to spend the night praying in the church with Dad's body. "Often, the oldest child will do so," he said, "as representative of the family." I had not heard of that custom and considered staying up. Then I decided to decline his offer. I thought that I had better get some sleep if I was to get through the next day, filled as it would be with giving the talk on my father and entertaining people who had come to the funeral. I also remembered that Mom and I had spent the night before Dad died with him and concluded that that was what had really counted.

My family and I set out for the church Friday morning, about a half hour before the start of the funeral Mass. We wanted to say our last good-bye before everyone else arrived. "I can't believe," I told JoAnne on our walk over, "that it's less than four days since I received Dale's phone call!" The church was already beginning to fill. We had left the coffin open for those who had not been able to attend the wake or prayer service. As we once again began to greet relatives and friends, I was increasingly awed at the number of people, over four hundred, who had come to share our grief. The realization hit me, as I watched them file by the casket with somber faces and not a few with tears in their eyes, how much my father and mother meant to these people and how many friends they had. Some had come from Edgeley, the town that in my childhood I associated with so much happiness. Some came from Wyndmere and had been close friends of Dad's when he owned the bar. Others were from Fargo, where my parents had lived and worked before their retirement. The relatives were from as close as right across the street in Kensal to as far away as Florida and Arizona.

Looking into their faces, I recognized people that I hadn't seen in years, an intimate part of my parents' lives, and, I realized, of mine. I noticed one man, in particular, as he nudged his way through the crowd and asked several people where I could be found. People pointed him over in my direction, and as he turned toward me, I knew immediately that he was Arnie Puetz, a friend of Dad's who had always been kind to me in Wyndmere when I was home from the seminary. He came up, put his arms around me, and offered his condolences. Then he said with a broad smile, "You know, you're starting to look like your old man." He added, "Come and see me when this is over and you have a chance. We'll have a cup of coffee and talk."

As the bells tolled, I kissed Dad's cold forehead and whispered, "You were a good father; I love you and always will." Mom and Marybeth said their own good-byes, while Dale stood by silently. Then the casket was closed. Father Kuhn and the two servers took their place at its foot. A long, white cloth was draped across it, a reminder of my father's baptism and of our hope in his resurrection. Father Kuhn welcomed everyone in our family's name, blessed the coffin, and the funeral liturgy began. Once the coffin had been pushed up the aisle by the pallbearers and situated next to the tall Easter candle with its burning flame, we took our places in the front pews. Because of the circular shape of the church, the first pew was relatively small, so Mom sat with Dale, Cindy, and Kaylie, while Marybeth and Jim sat with my family in the second pew.

After the opening prayer, my brother walked to the lectern for the first reading. Dale was obviously uncomfortable. I admired him for his willingness to be the first in front of everyone when he was under such stress. He read slowly and clearly from the Book of Wisdom, the passage confirming that "the souls of the virtuous are in the hands of God" and that, like "sparks run through the stubble," they will "shine out" (Wis 3:1-7). When he had returned to the pew and a short response was sung, JoAnne got up and moved to the lectern. She read from the Book of Revelation, for me one of the most meaningful scripture passages, about a new heaven and a new earth and the compassion of God: "Then I heard a loud voice call from the throne, 'You see this city? Here God lives among his people. He will make his home among them; ... he will wipe away all tears from their eyes'" (Rev 21:1-5). My wife's voice cracked midway through the reading, reminding me of how much she loved my father, and of how much I loved her.

The gospel reading was from St. Matthew, the words of Jesus on the Mount of the Beatitudes about the gift of happiness that can be found in the midst of suffering and sorrow (Matt 5:1-12). Father Kuhn's homily followed. What many of us found most moving was his description of my parents when he first met them. "I came to Edgeley as a newly-ordained priest," he told the congregation, "only to discover that in this first parish of mine there was already a dynamic group of lay leaders, two of whom were Ed and Elaine Sellner. Long before Vatican II's emphasis on the laity, they were actively involved at the Church of the Transfiguration, enriching other people's lives. I learned from them about the meaning of faith, hope, and love." And then he added, smiling broadly, "Ed heard more confessions than me or any of the other priests!"

Listening to Father Kuhn, I grew increasingly apprehensive about my own talk. I wanted to do a good job for Dad, but I was still nervous at whether I could get through it all without crying or creating a scene. My anxiety only increased as the rest of the Eucharist unfolded. Finally, after communion, the altar was cleared. I climbed the steps and stood behind the lectern and microphone. As I looked out over the crowded church, I realized that I was staring at a microcosm of my father's life, that all those people staring back at me had mysteriously been touched by my father and he by them. I wanted to speak for them and for my own family; to name their experiences and to highlight important aspects of Dad's life. I wanted to somehow convey what they already knew to be true: that my father's love had made a difference, and that his life had significance.

I began my talk hesitantly, stumbling over the first words as I thanked everyone for coming to share our family's sorrow. "Each of us remembers my father," I continued, "in different ways: his working in Edgeley, Wyndmere, and Fargo; his relaxing in Florida, Texas, or Arizona; his tending a garden and feeding birds in Kensal; his standing behind the bar fixing us a drink or at the door welcoming us home. He, quite simply, had a gift for making people feel at home—and in a world in which many feel unwelcome or like strangers, that gift of hospitality is one of the greatest gifts to have."

"The past few days seem like years," I acknowledged. "They have been filled with pictures and images and memories of Dad that come rushing out at unexpected moments." I referred to my own early memories of driving with my father in his truck and of his surprise gift of an electric train at Christmas. I mentioned how proud Dad had been when Dale won the state basketball championship, and of his love for Marybeth and her dogs. I spoke of my growing older "and finding that communication wasn't always easy between a father and a son." Then I told the congregation of the revelation that I had had two nights before, of seeing Dad "as if blinders had fallen from my eyes." I made specific reference to his tears: "Dad had tears in his eyes the day of his stroke. Twice that day, the first time when Dale joined Mom and Marybeth in the hospital room, and the second time when I arrived. The doctor told us that that was just a 'physical reaction' of some kind, since he 'really couldn't know that you were there.' I'm not so sure, however, that medical science has diagnosed the soul—nor acknowledged the reality of the heart. The tears, after all, were only there just after we each arrived."

"Ed Sellner," I spoke directly to my father, "you will be missed! And yet you have left each one of us a very rich heritage, the heritage of fond memories of you and of having no regrets *except one*: that we might have had more time on this earth with you."

I concluded: "You have taught us well, Dad, and we are grateful. And in our grief, which we will carry with us always in this life, we know that you are with God. We know too that you prepare a place for us when our own pilgrimages on this earth come to an end. You prepare a place *now*—through your example of a life well-lived. Thank you, Dad, and may you rest in peace, for your labors and love go before you."

I thought I noticed as I spoke that people seemed especially quiet and attentive when I mentioned Dad's and my difficulty in communicating.

Our families got into our cars following the final prayers at Mass and waited for the others to enter theirs. No one had much to say. The only sound was the slamming of car doors as people got in and prepared to leave. Once the hearse was in place, we followed it out to the cemetery. The long line of cars stirred up clouds of dust as we entered the dry grounds, but it had turned out to be a beautiful summer day. The wide expanse of blue sky was filled with broad swaths of cumulus white clouds, which kept the heat down. My mother, her children, and grandchildren gathered around the open grave and waited for the pallbearers to lift the casket from the hearse and carry it the short distance to the bier.

We stood there, reluctant observers in a state of suspended animation, watching the ritual unfold. I looked around, feeling as if in some sort of fog, and realized that the others in my family too were attempting to deal with this same sense of unreality. Most of us had seen funerals of the famous on television or the evening news; each of us had been participants in other funerals, watching as others grieved their loss. Now we uneasily found ourselves as the key actors in this drama of mourning, aware, despite our continuing state of denial, that it was our turn to model for others what they themselves would someday face. We stood there, my mother, sister, brother, and our families, huddled together in silence, bearing the weight of our loss, trying to comprehend the incomprehensible. Bewildered and confused, I noticed that others were also affected, including Uncle Wendy, who was struggling with the coffin as he and the other pallbearers carried it to the bier. He stumbled and almost fell into the open grave. I reached out to grab him, but he regained his balance just in time.

Memories of other burials flooded my mind as I waited for everyone to join us. I remembered the funeral of Grandpa John, whose body was the first to be carried here at a time in early autumn when much of the wheat and corn in the nearby fields had already been harvested. That day too, I thought, had been filled with sunshine as the patriarch of our family was laid to rest. Then, years later, came Grandma Mary's funeral in the midst of the winter snows. Following the prayers at that burial we had all quickly piled back into our cars to escape the cold and left her bronze casket, covered with flowers, gleaming in the stark stillness of the winter landscape. Standing there now, not far from where the two of them were buried, I remembered Grandma's stories of coming out to this prairie wilderness with Grandpa on their honeymoon, and of her first years of loneliness when the only visitors were friendly American Indians occasionally dropping by. Grandpa John passed on to us his own stories about the Great Depression and the green swarms of grass-hoppers that filled the air, blocking out the sun, destroying everything in their path. The two of them, I thought as I stood there silently, were truly pioneers in the vastness of this Dakota Territory. The only thing that kept them going was their courage, their persistence, their love.

I remembered my own early visits to see them as a child. One Christmas I sat in the back seat of the car with my cousin Barbara, both of us wrapped warmly in blankets, as my dad drove us and Mom through a snowstorm to get to my grandparents' farm. I remembered the vast dome of the sky that night, when the snow had stopped falling, and how it sparkled with the brightness of uncounted stars. I thought of another time, when I was older, and Dad had gotten stuck in snow outside of Kensal with Grandma Mary. Mom and I were mad that all of us, including Grandma, had to get out and push.

Now Dad was being buried in the same cemetery as my grandparents, a short ways out of Kensal, the town that he had come to call his own. It had not been the sheep ranch to which he had once said he wanted to retire. It was, however, a comfortable place to entertain relatives and friends.

Once all the mourners were out of their cars and had joined us near the grave, Kathy started the hymn "Holy God We Praise Thy Name," which was, she said, my father's favorite. Most of us adults were familiar with the words of this old, traditional hymn, and we sang them with conviction. Father Kuhn blessed the coffin with holy water one last time and invited each family member to do the same. We passed the silver sprinkler around, shaking it quickly over the casket. Then, joining hands, we prayed the Our Father. When we concluded, a long pause followed in which no one moved.

Suddenly the silence was interrupted by a blast of rifle shots which made us all jump, startled by the noise. It was the honor guard, firing their rifles into the air, in honor of Dad's military service during World War II. I heard Aunt Mary Lorraine cry out, "Look at all the birds," and as I raised my eyes from the coffin, I noticed for the first time how many had collected in the trees and on the telephone wires. At the sharp sound of the guns, they had flown up into the open sky, filling it with their wings. I stared at them dumbly, too dazed by the sound and the events of the last few days. Only later did I recall that there had been no birds in the cemetery when I had gone out to choose my father's burial site, nor were they there the day after the funeral when I walked out to visit the grave. Others commented at the reception after the burial how they had noticed the masses of birds mysteriously gathering with us in the cemetery that morning, how they had chirped loudly and seemed to watch the proceedings as if they too had come to pay their last respects.

One of the military men started to play taps. We stood
quietly listening to the mournful sound as it echoed through
the graves and trees and out beyond the cemetery to the
vastness of the prairie. Then, with Dan Lisko guiding them
through the rite, two of the men folded the flag that had
covered the casket. When that was done my uncle Bill took the
flag and handed it to me. I turned to my mother and placed it
gently in her hands. She had already cried during taps, and
now began to cry even more. I put my arms around her to help
alleviate some of her pain. John and Daniel huddled with her
too, concerned about their grandmother and visibly shaken by
all that had occurred so suddenly in their young lives. Almost
everyone was crying or had tears in their eyes when taps were
played. As everyone turned to leave, I reached out and rested
my hand on the coffin one last time. "Peace, Dad," I said
quietly, "and thank you."

We returned to the church and the large dining hall
attached to it. I was amazed that afternoon and evening how
much life and laughter there could be in the midst of so much
grief. At the lunch, which the women of the parish had
prepared, I heard more stories about my dad. Wally, one of
Dad's closest friends, said how much he appreciated being
asked to be a pallbearer. "Your dad had many friends," he told
me, "but I lost the best friend I ever had."

Later that afternoon relatives and family friends came over
to the house where we continued to eat, drink, and reminisce.
I acted as bartender, mixing drinks as my father would have
done. At one point, I took my father-in-law, Mel, out to the
front yard and showed him the ruts that were still visible in the
ground. I told him the story of Dad's and my last fight, and
then about my Dad's last words to me on the phone the
weekend before he died. My father-in-law had not been close
to his own father, and as we turned away from the marks in
the earth, he said to me, "I wish I had had that with my dad."

CHAPTER V

The Sense of Finality

We know that by the death of a brother or someone dear to us, the recollection of our coldness
and carelessness has sometimes aroused in us a
healthy fervor of spirit.

—John Cassian

TWO DAYS LATER JOHN, DANIEL, AND I told Mom and Marybeth
good-bye and prepared to leave for the ride back to St. Paul.
JoAnne had left with her parents the day before. I hugged my
mother, both of us in tears, crying for Dad and for each other.
The woman who used to take me in her arms to comfort me
as a child when I was afraid of the dark or had scraped my knee,
I now held. I did not want to leave her so soon after Dad's
burial, but she had insisted that JoAnne and I go with the boys
on the vacation we had promised our sons long before this
sudden death in the family. We had invited her to accompany
us, but she declined, citing the correspondence and legal
matters to which she had to attend. She was also adamant that,
following the family trip, I should go to Ireland for research I
was doing on a book about the Celtic saints and for my talk on
John Cassian at Oxford. I was definitely not enthused about
my planned journey abroad. In fact, I had decided at one point
that I would definitely not go. But besides my mother, my uncle
Bill and even JoAnne insisted that I not change my plans. Still,
I was genuinely concerned about my mother's emotional
health. I told her that I would wait and see how she was doing
before finally deciding about the European trip.

As she waved good-bye from the same spot where Dad and she had always stood together, my mother seemed suddenly frail, vulnerable, alone. I felt anguished leaving her that way. I felt torn between two loyalties: to my mother and to my wife and sons. The only rationalization that assuaged my guilt somewhat was knowing that Marybeth was staying with her, and that I would return when she might need me even more than now.

The ride back to St. Paul with John and Daniel covered the same route in reverse that I had made only a few days before. It went quickly, but as I pulled up in front of our house on Princeton Avenue I felt as if years had passed since that earlier trip. The same white house greeted us, in need of yet another coat of paint since Dad's and Mom's work on it a few summers earlier. The same elm and oak trees were growing in the front yard, minus a few twigs and branches that had fallen, as usual, while we were gone. The same lawn was visible, only now with the grass much longer due to recent rainfall. These were all familiar scenes, but I sensed immediately that nothing was the same.

I brought in the suitcases, kissed JoAnne, and asked her how her trip back had gone. We talked for a while about it and what had yet to be done before leaving on our vacation. I glanced through the mail in the kitchen and then headed for my study on the second floor. From there, I climbed the steps to the attic on the third floor and pushed back the heavy wooden door at the top of the stairs. I began rummaging through boxes and stacks of old magazines, looking for a photo album from my childhood. I was searching for a picture of Dad and me, taken when I was only about nine months old, an image of the two of us that kept coming to my mind as I drove from Kensal back to St. Paul. In a box, underneath newspapers that I had been saving from the Kennedy years, I found the album and opened its faded cover.

At first, as I flipped through the pages, I couldn't believe my eyes. There they were, all the relatives I had just seen at

Dad's funeral! Only, in the pictures, they are much younger, their faces without wrinkles, untouched as yet by the physical changes that time brings. I stared down with amazement at the photographs of my aunts and uncles who, as young adults, are holding my cousins and me in their arms or by the hand. Smiles light their faces, and they are obviously enjoying our baby years—despite the disruptions, not to mention dirty diapers, that have entered their lives. One of the pictures shows just us children, eight cousins, in front of a short, spindly Christmas tree at Grandpa's and Grandma's house on the farm. We seem to have been piled together randomly on the floor. Grandpa John in his bib overalls is seated on the edge of a chair, overseeing the confusion. He has a look of bewilderment on his face, as if he does not know what to do with all these new arrivals. The tree in the picture reminded me of the story Mom would tell about when she was a child. My grandfather one Christmas had suddenly grabbed their little tree, all decorated with candles and homemade decorations, and tossed it out the front door into the yard. Its dry branches had turned into a bright burning torch, set afire by one of the candles. Upset by the loss as well as amazed at their father's quickness, Mom and her brothers and sisters had watched from the window as the flames roared, lighting up the night.

In another picture my uncle Leland stands in the yard on my grandparents' farm and holds me, a two-year-old child. He was the uncle I had started calling Daddy the time I had stayed with Grandpa and Grandma while my parents were getting their grocery business started in the Twin Cities after World War II. Those first days without my parents had seemed like a bad dream—as if I had entered a dark tunnel. I could recall nothing except being physically sick, confused, and depressed, not knowing where Mom and Dad were. Days or weeks later, emerging from the tunnel, I remember holding onto Grandma's hand and being carried around by Uncle Leland.

I turned the pages of the album, intent upon finding that particular photo of my father and me. There it was: Dad has his army uniform on and is holding me, a baby, in one hand, up to the camera, while the other hand supports my neck and back. I am dressed in what appears to be a light, summer outfit, and my head rests against Dad's cheek. He is smiling broadly, and I too have a smile on my face, though my eyes are not focused on the camera but on someone outside of the picture, over to the left. Probably my mother.

I gazed at that picture of my father and me for some time. Tears ran down my cheeks and I began to sob, so intense were the feelings of loss that overwhelmed me. I cried not only over the loss of my father, whom I loved more than I had known, but over the loss of my childhood. I cried because I could never go back to those days, to being a child, *my father*'s child. I felt as if I had entered that dark tunnel once again, and that my link, at least a very special link with the past, had been severed.

I wiped my tears on my sleeves and pulled the picture from the album. Carrying it downstairs to my study, I put it in the frame with another of Dad holding my son, John, on his knees. In each picture, with son and grandson, Dad is smiling.

The following day JoAnne did the laundry, I cut the grass, and the four of us frantically repacked our suitcases to go on vacation. Late in the afternoon, tired and hot, we climbed into the car and headed south. We had originally planned a leisurely week's drive through southern Minnesota, Iowa, Indiana, and Missouri, and then back home again. Our main stops were to be in Springfield, Illinois, and New Harmony, Indiana, historical places that we hoped the boys would enjoy. As it turned out, the trip was not relaxing, and the only happy time that we really had was the day we spent at an amusement park in Santa Claus, Indiana, forgetting momentarily the events of the preceding week. There was simply no pretending that we could easily put Dad's death behind us. Instead our days and nights were filled with memories, tensions, and tears as each of us began to deal with the reality that Dad was not coming back.

This sense of finality was even more painful than the original experience of loss. At least before there had been the activity of preparing for Dad's funeral and greeting the people who came to Kensal to share our grief. Now, on this trip, even though it took us far from familiar sites, there was this horrific vacuum caused by his absence and the intensifying awareness that, in this life, we would never see him again. That was the hardest thing of all. No activities on our trip could fill these intense feelings of emptiness. At the same time, there was the paradox that although Dad was dead, he was not gone. Almost anything might remind us of him and of our loss.

On the first full day of our trip, at a restaurant some-where in Illinois, I embarrassed myself and startled the waitress by suddenly breaking into tears over lunch. John had surprised us by saying, "I hope when I grow up that I have as many friends as Grandpa Ed." JoAnne had smiled and said, "What a wonderful thought." Then both boys and their mother turned to me. The grief, suddenly exposed, was difficult to hide. Both boys looked disconcerted to see their father cry, and while John leaned over and patted my shoulder, Dan got up from his chair and gave me a hug. We took turns that week comforting each other.

Throughout that day, and at other times during our vaca-tion, grief kept reappearing, along with reminders of my father. I thought I saw Dad that first day when an older couple, a gray-haired man and woman, drove by us on the highway in a large silver car, shining with lots of chrome. From the back the man looked a lot like Dad, although as I told JoAnne, "If it is Dad, he's got another wife—and an even bigger car!" By the time we arrived in Springfield late that afternoon, after a short visit to the village of New Salem, we were tired and hungry. We checked into a motel immediately, and then without supper (a fatal mistake!) went in search of the house where Lincoln had once lived before becoming President.

There, at the restored two-story home on Eighth and
Jackson Street, we encountered another man who reminded
me of my father. He and his wife, along with another couple,
were part of the tour that began early in the evening. This
older man, quite tall and heavyset, did not look at all like my
dad. It was his limp that caught my attention, the way he
walked so gingerly on one foot as we passed from room to
room. I recalled Dad's visit to our home earlier that spring,
and how, when I had taken him and Mom out for lunch, he
tried so hard to keep up with us. His foot was giving him
trouble. Now, glancing at this stranger with his limp, I wished
that I had been more sensitive to Dad's difficulty and simply
slowed down. That was the first of the regrets that only
increased as time passed.

Dad appeared too in my response to Daniel's tiredness and
grief. While I was enthused about seeing Lincoln's home once
more, remembering that Dad, Mom, and I had seen it for the
first time exactly twenty-five years before, John and Daniel were
considerably less impressed. They had not cared at all for New
Salem, where the young Lincoln had lived for six years and
been postmaster. They called its winding streets, restored log
cabins, and numerous little shops "boring" and just wanted to
get back in the car. As we were touring the Lincoln house in
Springfield, they continued to mutter and gripe. Even when
our guide pointed out that Lincoln's sons were the same age
as ours when they moved into the White House, John and
Daniel looked away and yawned.

Coming out of the house after the tour, I had had enough
of their irritability and obvious lack of interest in Lincoln, a
man who had long been a hero of mine. When I told them to
act a little more appreciative, I got only a sullen look from John
and a smart remark from Daniel. I lost my temper and told the
latter to be quiet. Tired and hungry, like me, Daniel reacted
verbally, using language that my father had once corrected me
about. By that time, I, of course, felt compelled to defend the
memory of Dad and uphold his instructions to me about "bad

mouths." Things went from bad to worse. I finally gave Daniel a good swat on his behind and walked away with John in tow, while Daniel stayed with his mother. When all of our tempers had cooled a bit, and we had eaten, I realized how much my own expression of anger was like my father's and how irrational it might appear to a child.

All of us were exhausted by the time we got back to the motel. We expressed our tiredness and grief in different ways. John had cried earlier when we told him what motel we were going to stay in, wanting a more modern one that had a video arcade. Daniel, after enraging me, enraged his mother by throwing the keys to our motel room into the swimming pool. The two of them watched the keys sink to the bottom of the pool at its deepest end. We were not a happy lot that night.

The next morning, in the motel that John had called old and ugly, I awoke before the others and went into the bathroom to read. Once again I was overcome with emotion. I reached for a towel to smother the noise of my crying so as not to awaken JoAnne and the boys. Being back in a town so much associated with Lincoln, I recalled the short vacation the boys, my parents, and I had taken three years before to the Black Hills of South Dakota, where Lincoln's face is carved into Mount Rushmore. For the first time, as I cried in that motel room in Springfield, I heard more than anger behind my dad's harsh words to me on that earlier trip.

It was the first week of August 1988. Conscious at midlife that my parents weren't going to live forever, I had planned that short vacation with them so that we could be together while JoAnne had a little time to herself. At the end of the month I was to leave for England and Ireland to do research into the Early Celtic Church and its spirituality.

The time together that week with my parents and sons had gone well, but, as usual, we tried to cover more territory than we should have. There was a lot of driving to do, and I was the one who did most of it. In order to make time, we decided to return from the Black Hills to Kensal in one day, covering more than seven hundred miles. All of us were crammed into my Toyota, getting increasingly tired and on each other's nerves. Dad, of course, had mentioned how much room there would have been in *his* car. We had just left a pizza place in a little town in South Dakota when my son John asked, "Where is my canteen?" It was the canteen that I had given him as a souvenir of our trip. None of us could find it, and I immediately blamed John, angry at his forgetfulness. This was not the first time he had forgotten something or other since we had left St. Paul.

In the car, I kept asking him how he could have forgotten the canteen. I berated him until he finally blurted out, "That hurts—you're hurting me," and began to cry.

My Dad sat there beside me in the front seat—ominously quiet. Then he asked, "Do you want my opinion on the subject?"

I looked at him and saw the anger in his eyes. I met his gaze and snapped back defensively, "Stay out of it." Then I angrily drove back to the restaurant and picked up the canteen. We were on the road again when Dad suddenly exploded, "You don't have to treat him that way! What kind of example are you giving?"

I replied instantly, enraged and threatened by his outburst, "Stay out of it! And don't correct me in front of my sons!"

Dad yelled back, "I will never go on a trip with you again. All we ever do is fight."

I drove on, still mad at John and now at my father, tired from driving, and feeling guilty about our exchange. I was especially hurt at Dad's words about never going with me on a trip again. Here he was, I thought, once again giving me little credit for my efforts. Finally I spoke up, as John had just done with me minutes before, "You hurt me! I was the one who suggested this trip. I was the one who wanted to spend more time with you and Mom. It really has been a good trip up till now."

Silence followed. The only sounds in the car were John's muffled sobs and my mother's crying. I remembered the angry encounter between Dad and me years before over the length of my hair, and how she had tried to mediate. Now she said nothing. This time, however, it was not just an argument between father and son; it was three generations of Sellner males trying to work out their differences. Daniel didn't help matters by saying to me, "You made Grandma cry."

By the time we reached my parents' home in Kensal, in the early hours of the morning, Dad was apologizing to me for his angry remark. It was the first time I remembered him saying, "I'm sorry." I also was asking forgiveness of him, and of my oldest son. By that time John did not know what was going on; he had fallen asleep and was just waking up.

Later that morning, after all of us had had some sleep, I was in the kitchen with Mom. "I'm sorry for my behavior last night," I told her, "but I'm still puzzled by the anger toward John that possessed me. I didn't know that I had such high expectations of my firstborn. I was treating him as if he should act much older—or as if he shouldn't make mistakes at all."

Without thinking, my mother responded, "Well, that's how your father always treated you—as much as I tried to tell him that you were only a child."

When I heard her say that, it was as if something inside me clicked; I recognized how I had fallen into an inherited pattern. With that realization I felt a sense of liberation, of freedom from my past. Now I had some choices in raising my own sons. I didn't have to be controlled by my unconscious. At the same time, I did not at all blame my father for what was wrong with me. Rather, I wondered what patterns Dad had inherited from his father, and what high expectations he had of himself, and thus of me, his firstborn son. I could, I thought that morning, try to break the pattern and, by becoming more accepting of myself, save John and Daniel from a cycle of self-hatred and self-blame.

Back in the Springfield hotel, as I attempted to muffle my tears in the towel, I recalled what had happened later that fall, after the trip to the Black Hills, when I had arrived in England to do my research. The revelation of Dad's positive qualities that I had had the night before my father's wake had its origins in the awareness of how much I had always blamed my father for so many things.

I was on a train from Oxford to northern England where I was to stay for a few days with an ecumenical community. Watching the countryside rush by with its acres of lush, green meadows filled with flocks of grazing sheep, that incident with my father and John in the car on our return from the Black Hills kept coming back to me. Alone, cut off from family and friends, I felt terrifically lonely. I was missing them, and feeling especially remorseful about Dad's and my fight. As I looked up from a book and stared out the windows of the train, I was struck with the realization that all of my life—or at least since I was an adolescent—I had been critical of my father. Some of this was possibly due to my fear of him and some of his hurtful remarks to me as a child. A lot of it had to do with not being sure that he loved me. As I had read once in a sermon by Lutheran theologian Paul Tillich, "We cannot love where we feel rejected. We are hostile toward that to which we belong and by whom we feel judged." I had, I knew, felt judged by my father, a judgment that had led to anger and a lot of hurt. But on that train headed north I also comprehended that Dad perhaps had never been sure of *my* love, precisely because I had been so critical of him—critical because he had not had the advantages of an education that I had had; critical that he had been "only a bartender," a man living in a small town, a man who didn't know all that much about history or about other countries and other places.

I couldn't believe how judgmental I had been, how full of pride, how obnoxious! For years I had never really given him credit for being a good father, for his long hours of work, for his sense of responsibility, for his personal integrity. I remembered the conversation he and I had once had when he told me that during the many years behind the bar he had never developed a foul mouth or been unfaithful to my mother. Sitting on the train with the English countryside rushing past, I recognized, finally, that those were the things that really mattered—not educational achievements, financial status, or where one lived. Like the prodigal son, I knew I needed to ask forgiveness of my father—not only for expecting him to be a perfect parent but for overlooking all that he had accomplished in his own right.

When I returned home that November I looked for the opportunity. Dad and Mom were visiting us for Thanksgiving, and the morning after, as Mom and Dad and I sat for a moment alone in the kitchen with JoAnne upstairs and the boys watching cartoons in the family room, I turned to both of my parents, and said: "I want you to know how sorry I am for any hurt I've caused you." They looked at me without saying a word, surprised by my confession, not knowing what to say. "I'm sorry," I continued, "but I realized while I was gone how much I expected you to be without faults, and how often I blamed you for my own unhappiness. Now I know you've been good parents, loving parents all my life. And I love you." My remarks were directed mostly at my father.

My mother, of course, responded, "But you've always been a good son and made us proud." Dad nodded, but said nothing. I noticed, however, that he had tears in his eyes, once again. It was as if he understood what I had been trying to communicate, as if he'd forgiven me long before I ever knew to ask.

Now, as I wiped my own tears in the Springfield motel, I remembered that trip to the Black Hills with Dad and its aftermath. For the first time I heard the hurt behind his angry words to me, "All we ever do is fight." While I had been feeling hurt and rejected *again* when I heard him say that in the car, I now realized that he had been hurt as much as I had been by our years of fighting. For too long I had thought that I was the only one in pain.

I cried that morning in Springfield, wondering how I could have missed this dynamic and others over the years. I cried until my forehead throbbed with pain, until I could cry no more. I was filled with regret, a bitter remorse for all the unkind things I ever did or said. I kept asking myself as I sobbed into the towel: "Why? Why did it take me so long before I recognized the goodness of my father? Why did I allow such petty things to stand in our way?" I was sorry for what I had done: for all the arguments, harsh words, and years of silence that had kept us apart. I was sorry too for what I had failed to do: for my lack of sensitivity toward my father, for not hearing or understanding when he complained so frequently about his work, for not spending that last morning with him at our house, for the fact that until his death I had not even been aware of the color of his eyes.

I wanted to undo and remake the past. I wanted him back so that we could start all over. I wanted to make amends for the time that had been lost between us. Most of all I wanted to see him again, to see his face as I had at his surprise birthday party, to look into his eyes, reflecting back knowledge that I loved him and that he loved me. "Why?" I asked God. "Why did he die at a point when he and I had just become so close, when we had finally grown to trust our love for each other, when my own sons were appreciating his presence in their lives?"

I knew that a turning point in our relationship had been reached somewhere between the Black Hills and my train ride in England; somewhere between my asking forgiveness of him in our kitchen at Thanksgiving and the last battle in Kensal in May when we finally had laid down our arms. It had taken us a while to reach that point, our last night together, of simply sitting in our family room and enjoying each other's company. That was the hardest part of all to accept. That's why I felt so much regret. I cried knowing that at the time I was just beginning to get to know him, my father died.

As I stood there in the bathroom, alone with my grief and regret, aware of this awful sense of finality, something else entered my thoughts, something even more unsettling in its irrationality than I had previously imagined. "What if," I asked myself, "*I* caused Dad's sudden death?"

I put the towel down and stared into space, horrified at this latest thought. Wasn't I the one who believed firmly in the efficacy of prayer? Hadn't I the very morning I received the phone call from Dale prayed for Dad and Mom, prayed that they have long and happy life? But, adding, as I prayed,"If they aren't going to be happy, don't let it be long."

I was amazed at my own presumption. "Of course, I didn't want either of them to suffer, but what right," I asked myself, "did I have to make such a prayer? What right do I have to pray for certain conditions regarding anyone's longevity? It's really not up to me what conditions should be present when a person dies. That's up to God, and happiness may be no criterion."

God, I knew, had answered my prayers many times before, including the one on my way to Fargo that I be with Dad if he had to die. Now I wondered if perhaps God, hearing my petition the morning before my father's stroke, had taken Dad from us.

This dialogue with myself, irrational and highly-charged, went through my head and added to the confusion I was feeling. What became clear that morning, however, was that I had lied to everyone at Dad's funeral, especially myself, when I preached that I had no regrets. I was filled with tremendous regrets, especially that time had run out for my father, for us.

"We do suffer for our sins," I thought, "especially those against our parents. Every vicious word and unkind deed comes back to haunt us. Sin is its worst punishment."

That morning in Springfield I felt as the fourth-century desert mother Pelagia did when she confessed to her soul friend Nonnus, "I know my sins; they are heavier than the sands of the sea."

CHAPTER VI

Resetting Broken Bones

> A brother asked Abba Poemen what he should
> do about his sins. The old man said to him, "He
> who wishes to purify his faults purifies them with
> tears, and he who wishes to acquire virtues
> acquires them with tears."

WE LEFT SPRINGFIELD THAT SAME DAY after touring the offices where Lincoln had practiced law and the Old State Capital where he served in the legislature and delivered his famous "House Divided Against Itself" speech. We felt divided ourselves, tired and listless. The visit to Lincoln's tomb at Oak Ridge Cemetery before we left did not change our dispositions but only intensified our feelings of grief. Death was everywhere.

We drove on toward New Harmony, Indiana, a small town hidden in the humid mists of southern Indiana. Despite the uncomfortable heat and my own intense feelings of regret and guilt, I began to experience some consoling resources for grieving. Besides the patience and compassion of JoAnne, and the obvious love of my sons for their grandfather and for me, I found comfort in music. My wife had surprised me with a cassette tape as a gift to take with me on our journey south, and while I listened to the songs I found myself calmed unexpectedly. The pain of loss was not taken away, but it was made a bit more tolerable by the music that filled our car. I also discovered that the landscape itself seemed to have a tremendous healing effect on my troubled soul. The route we took to New Harmony was on back roads, through rural America. The fields of golden wheat, rows of ripening corn, and old, wooden bridges mysteriously offered solace. The spirit of the land seemed to meet my troubled spirit, soothe it gently, and even strengthen it. The natural world, I was discovering, is a source of human comfort. Still, grief was never far away.

We pulled in to New Harmony late in the afternoon, and headed straight for the New Harmony Inn. Both town and inn were famous for their historical and religious associations. The town was once the home of two of the earliest experimental communes in the United States: the Rappites, a religious group from Germany; and the Owenites, a group of educators and intelligentsia. Neither nineteenth-century community had been successful, but by the 1960s many of the original buildings were restored. A labyrinth consisting of shrubbery-lined paths leading to a temple at the center was also redone on the edge of town. First constructed by the Rappites, it symbolized, according to a postcard, "the difficult choices one must make during life and the reward for those who do not despair." Along with a new cultural center to celebrate New Harmony's past, a beautiful Roofless Church had been built, quite literally without a roof, almost in the middle of a cornfield. Under arches at one end there was a modern statue of the Virgin Mary called "Descent of the Holy Spirit." Jewish artist Jacques Lipchitz had created it, he said, "for the good of all mankind that the spirit might prevail."

Other features of New Harmony were a park, dedicated to Paul Tillich, and a wayside shrine in honor of Thomas Merton. The New Harmony Inn itself seemed more like a retreat house than a motel. A small, round chapel was attached to the main lodge with Eastern Orthodox icons of Mary and the saints, including the wisdom figures from the desert Christians, on its walls. A large swimming pool behind the inn had a roof which could be drawn back on sunny days to catch the warmth of the sun's rays and to reveal a clear view of the summer sky. The grounds of the New Harmony Inn were planted profusely with flowers: purple delphiniums, blue morning glories, pink petunias, white daisies, red and pink roses, and brightly-colored fuchsias.

Besides the historical and religious associations, there were personal ones that had drawn us to New Harmony. I had first visited the town while a doctoral student at Notre Dame in the mid-1970s. I had been studying Tillich's writings at the time and was impressed by the breadth of his vision and the depth of his thought; by his ability to relate culture, history, and psychology to theology. I had read in a biography that Tillich's ashes had been scattered in the grove bordering a reflecting pool in New Harmony. Aware that our lives can be strangely touched when we visit the graves of those we respect or love, I had wanted to make a kind of pilgrimage there. Following my first visit, I had gone back to New Harmony on other occasions, fascinated by the spirituality of the place. In 1978 I took JoAnne there and, at the center of the Labyrinth, a place associated with "right choices," I asked her to marry me. For both of us New Harmony was very special. We had wanted to return someday and to share it with our children. Now, at last, we had brought our sons, but under less than harmonious circumstances.

We checked in at the main desk of the inn, and within minutes all four of us were splashing in the swimming pool. Its cool, refreshing waters helped alleviate some of the tiredness and strain of our long, hot drive. An hour later we took the boys to dinner at the Red Geranium, a popular restaurant near the inn. The boys did not appreciate its leisurely atmosphere, nor were the adult customers especially enamored of them. Neither JoAnne nor I had a relaxing time. JoAnne sat patiently listening to John's complaints at the slow service ("McDonalds is a lot faster"), while I took

Daniel for a walk to get him to stop playing with the silverware. By the time he and I returned, my steak was cold. He, of course, disliked his hamburger ("too fancy").

When we got back to our room, I phoned my mother to find out how she was doing and to let her know that we had reached New Harmony. I could tell by her voice that the sense of finality was also affecting her. I listened as she told of each day's activities since we had left, and I tried to console her when she cried. "I know, Mom, it's hard," I said. Neither of us felt very good. She was experiencing the new, raw feelings of loneliness, and I was feeling the effects of regret and guilt, wondering if I was somehow responsible for Dad's death. "We love you, Mom," I told her before handing the phone over to JoAnne.

After JoAnne and the boys had taken their turns talking with my mother and had hung up, I decided to go for a walk. JoAnne wanted to do some reading, and John and Daniel were happy to watch television.

I headed straight for the Thomas Merton shrine, located not far from the Roofless Church. Merton had long been a significant spiritual mentor for me. I had first read his autobiography, *Seven Storey Mountain*, when I was twelve years old, and I immediately identified with his quest for holiness and God, his love of spirituality. I wanted to give my life to God as he had done. On some level too he functioned, through his writings, as a spiritual father for me at a time when I was beginning to feel alienated from Dad. So I had followed Merton's example and joined the seminary to study for the priesthood. Even when I discerned that celibacy was not my call, his ideals and writings continued to influence me. In graduate school at Notre Dame, when I had first begun to pay attention to my dreams and the messages they contained, it was Merton who appeared as my guide in one of the most vivid.

In the dream I am standing on a ridge, overlooking circular buildings in a valley far below. Each building is connected by what appear to be passageways, forming a mandala, a symbol of wholeness. At my side is Merton who, in gesturing toward them, says, "This is the church as it's meant to be," and then, pointing to another part of the valley, says, "and over there is the church that didn't adapt." In the direction that he points I see the same circular objects, but they are not connected, and a blustering, cold wind blows through their shattered windows and empty rooms.

With the help of Fritz, my spiritual director (a Lutheran pastor trained in Jungian psychology), I understood that this crucial dream had a number of levels of meaning. On one level it spoke of my need to acknowledge and integrate various aspects of myself into greater harmony. On another level it contained my vision of the church and how it too must change if it is to survive. Later I came to see the dream as reflecting my own life-work—the drive for psychological wholeness and personal holiness, and the quest for Christian unity. I appreciated that it was Merton who in the dream stood there on the ridge, at the crossroads, where wisdom is often found. Other mentors had come along, especially Robert Kennedy when I was in college. But Merton, my contemplative side, stayed with me through very active years of discerning my vocation, marrying, finishing my doctorate, finding employment, raising a family. It was he, the writer within me, who prompted me finally to begin to write books in the area of Christian spirituality. Because of him and what he represented, I had gone to England in 1988 to research Celtic and desert spiritual traditions, to study with the medieval scholar Benedicta Ward, an Anglican nun, and to live in Oxford at the St. Theosevia Centre for Christian Spirituality with a friend of Merton's, Canon Donald Allchin. I had hoped that some of Merton's wisdom would rub off on me, just by being in the presence of one of his own good friends.

Now, as I walked at dusk toward the Merton shrine in New Harmony, I noticed the soft glow of fireflies, flashing intermittently, lighting a path from the inn to the Red

Geranium. Across the street was the shrine. When I arrived, I could just barely make out, from the last streaks of sunset across the open sky, the medieval statue of Mary, Queen of Peace, with Jesus in her arms. Her smile, despite the fading light, was still visible under the rustic wooden canopy sheltering mother and child. I had come here before, but this was the first time at nightfall. My attention was caught by a large rectangular box near the base of the shrine, lit only by a small electrical bulb. I walked over and stared down at the words printed in calligraphy:

> As long as we are on earth, the love that unites us will bring us suffering by our very contact with one another, because this love is the resetting of a Body of broken bones.
> Even saints cannot live with saints on this earth without some anguish, without some pain at the differences that come between them.
> There are two things which men can do about the pain of disunion with other men. They can love or they can hate.
> Hatred recoils from the sacrifice and sorrow that are the price of this resetting of bones. It refuses the pain of reunion.

I had been thinking of my father on my walk over. Now before my eyes was a passage that spoke directly to my horrible predicament of feeling overwhelmed with regret and guilt.

I had read those words on other visits and had not paid much attention to them. My life experiences had not yet prepared me to comprehend their significance. I knew, however, that they were from Merton's *New Seeds of Contemplation*, and part of a longer passage that continued:

> And in so far as each one of us is lonely, is unworthy, each one hates himself. Some of us are aware of this self-hatred, and because of it reproach ourselves and punish ourselves needlessly. Others,

who are less conscious of their own self-hatred,
realize it in a different form by projecting it on to
others.
But love, by its acceptance of the pain of reunion,
begins to heal all wounds.

I needed to hear those words, to see them. And, in the
synchronicity of God's timing, there they were! They were
words of solace and of luminosity; words acknowledging that
no relationship is ever perfect, and that even between the
most loving people can be anguish and pain caused by their
differences. Once again, I thought to myself, Merton is acting
as my spiritual guide, assuring me that suffering and, yes,
grief itself, so much related to those we love, can be redemp-
tive, can become a way to transformation, to the resetting of
broken bones.

It would be months before I could begin fully to integrate
the wisdom of Merton's words, but I felt strangely calmed
that night. I was not only filled with a degree of consolation
but, in recalling aspects of the entire passage from Merton's
book, a clearer understanding of some of the dimensions of
my relationship with my father. I recognized that, like
everyone, at the core of my life was the struggle to feel
accepted, a constant battle for some measure of self-esteem
against self-doubts and feelings of self-rejection, self-con-
tempt. I, without knowing it, kept looking for acceptance
from outside myself, starting with my parents. I tried hard to
win that acceptance, especially from my father, projecting my
own feelings of unacceptability onto Dad, blaming him for
my own lack. Some of his early remarks and actions, of
course, had not helped. But neither did *my* projections. I now
realized that, while he had expected perfection from me as
a child, I had expected perfection *from him* as I grew older.
Resentment is the bitter fruit of expecting more from someone than he or she can give.

Standing there in front of Mary's statue, I couldn't pretend
to understand the mystery of my life and of my father's. All I

knew was that somehow, in our pain, our love for each other had bridged the gap between us, paradoxically, it seemed, when we stopped expecting more than the other could give. I turned and walked slowly back to the New Harmony Inn, not fully aware of the implications of Merton's other words about not punishing ourselves needlessly. Aspects of my grief would definitely include the agony—not of learning to forgive my father for things that he had done to me (I had already done that some time before); not even, as my mother would have to do, of learning to forgive God for having taken Dad from her. No, my grief process was to consist of learning to forgive myself—or, rather, of allowing a compassionate God and a loving father to show me that I had already been forgiven, and that I didn't have to continue beating myself with my own high perfectionistic standards.

The next morning, while the others slept, I wrote my mother a letter:

> August 1, 1991
> New Harmony, IN
>
> Dear Mom,
>   We arrived here yesterday about 4:30 p.m. and checked into the New Harmony Inn. It's been thirteen years since I asked JoAnne to marry me in the middle of the Labyrinth. I hoped then to find a level of "new harmony" within myself and with God. Now I feel that I have found some of that: a new sense of harmony and contentment with being married and having two wonderful sons who share my happiness and sorrow too. John and Daniel are good sons, thoughtful and sensitive. We are all, though, affected so much by the loss of Dad. Clearly the pain of that loss lies just below the surface—waiting to erupt whenever something reminds us of him. I can only guess at the feelings of loss you must feel after loving him a lifetime.

We will get through this time of grieving *together*,
Mom, and although we'll never stop missing Dad, he
would want us to experience happiness again. Especially you—some level of the happiness we experienced when the family was all together as
friends.

I love you with all of my heart,

Ed

P.S. JoAnne, John, and Daniel send their love.

When JoAnne and the boys awoke, I walked over to the
Red Geranium and brought back some pastries, coffee, and
juice for a quick breakfast. Then we were on the road to Santa
Claus Land. We spent the day in bright sunshine, surrounded
by other families, in an amusement part designed to look like
the North Pole. Amid Christmas trees and artificial snow we
played games, rode antique cars, and held each other tight on
the roller coaster rides. At least temporarily, memory of Dad's
death was put aside.

The following day we planned only to take a tour of New
Harmony and sit by the pool. We spent the morning going in
and out of the little shops along the main street and visiting
the New Harmony Museum, which housed a collection of
historical artifacts related to the town's early pioneers. Daniel
and John were most impressed with the old cannons in front
of the museum. At one of the bookstores I discovered a
quotation by Lillian Hellman. It was at the main desk near the
cash register and practically jumped out at me. The quotation
was on the cover of a set of literary postcards, and when I read
it I thought immediately of Dad's and my relationship: "People
change and forget to tell each other."

That evening, while John and Daniel ate pizza with a young
woman whom the inn had recommended as a sitter, JoAnne
and I went back to the Red Geranium for a quiet meal. I had
asked for a table in the Tillich Refectory, a dining area with
windows through which one could look out on a scenic view

of the surrounding Tillich Park and reflecting pool. I loved that room, for it was there that JoAnne and I had celebrated after my proposal to her thirteen years before. Along with the beautiful view and fond memories, I also loved the entrance to this room, the huge wooden doors carved with modern archetypal figures from the Hebrew and Christian scriptures: the Prophet and the Shepherd. They represented Tillich's understanding of the two types of religious leadership needed for today's churches: ministries that both challenge and support. They also represent, I thought as we sat down to eat, two aspects of parenting, of fatherhood.

JoAnne and I talked about the last few days of our vacation, and of my father's death. It was the first quiet time that the two of us had had for weeks. JoAnne did most of the listening that evening. I cried for both of my parents and for all the lost years between Dad and me. I wondered aloud how my mother would survive without Dad. I expressed, finally, my fear of having somehow caused Dad's death.

"What if, through my prayers, I did bring about his sudden death?" I asked JoAnne. "What if I am responsible? I know it sounds crazy, but I'm haunted by that fear."

JoAnne did not immediately respond. Then she set down her glass of wine, and replied calmly, gently, "No, Ed, God listens to our prayers, but God also decides what's best for us. He's not a puppet on a string."

Before falling asleep that night, I prayed for a dream that might shed light on my confusion and ambivalent feelings. I was aware that dreams had helped me in the past, and that certain places, even in ancient times, were associated with mystical enlightenment. What better place, I thought, than here in New Harmony, the landscape that reflects so much of my soul?

I awoke the next morning and tried to recall if I had had any dream. Nothing, not even a fragment. I was disappointed. I crawled from my bed, dressed quietly while the other three still slept, and went to get some coffee. I bought a cup at the restaurant and sat at an outdoor table sipping it slowly as I adjusted to another day—without my father. When I had finished the cup, I decided to go for one last walk over to the Roofless Church, Merton shrine, and through Tillich Park before our departure.

As I walked, the faint scent of the pink and white climbing roses on the picket fences mingled with the fine morning air. I greeted the groundkeepers, who were already out clipping shrubs and trimming grass. At the Merton shrine I paused briefly to pay my respects and watched a monarch butterfly dance among the flowers. Near the Roofless Church a brown rabbit awaited its mate. The grass glistened in the early morning sun, and a haze still lingered over the fields of corn. At the entrance to the park where Tillich's ashes had been scattered, I saw a dark rock carved with words from his writings:

> *Estranged and Re-united*
> *The New Being*

I could hear the rustle of leaves and the stir of life, the first sounds of birds chirping, echoing through the grove of pine trees on the farther bank. Near the placid waters at the edge of the reflecting pool stately willows wept. Stopping for a moment on the path leading to the clearing, I saw a chickadee. With its black head and throat and light body feathers, it was singing a clear, sweet song, pausing every now and then as if listening for a response from another part of the grove.

Ah, I thought, no messages from dreams, but the appearance of a bird and its beautiful singing. Dad would have appreciated that.

I walked on down to the water's edge, where a large black bust of Tillich had been placed, and read on another stone, much larger than the first, the following scriptural message:

> And he shall be like a tree planted by the rivers of water that bringeth forth his fruit, for his season, his leaf also shall not wither, and whatsoever he doeth shall prosper.

A sensation of profound quietude settled over me, a cessation for the moment of my struggles with all the restless demons that had fought for my attention the past week and over the years.

I returned to the inn and roused the boys. JoAnne was already up, reading. The boys and I got dressed for one last swim at the pool. JoAnne had decided to squeeze out a bit more solitude by staying behind. I followed the boys down the path to the pool and was happy to see that the roof had been pulled back to reveal the blue open sky above. Another father was there with his two sons, younger than mine, who from their appearance and accent seemed to be from India. While John and Daniel played at the shallower end of the pool, I began swimming laps. After the first couple, I did so with a deliberate intention: to ask God's forgiveness for my past sins. I swam forty-six laps that morning in the crystal blue waters of the pool, one for each year of my life. As I swam, I tried to remember what I was doing that year, and what I was sorry for. I prayed as I swam for forgiveness and for healing in my life. I prayed for all my loved ones, who had suffered from my blindness and selfishness. I prayed for the resetting of broken bones. Even as the laps increased, I did not mind the swim. Nor did I feel all that tired. I was reexperiencing my first baptism, and I knew that I would come forth from the waters reborn.

We stopped at the Labyrinth on the way out of town. It was not as I had remembered it. The green shrubs were overgrown now, the paths harder to distinguish, the temple in the middle in disrepair. Again, our sons were unimpressed. They did show interest, however, when I told them that I had proposed to their mother at the center where the winding paths joined.

Despite the brief interlude in New Harmony, we were exhausted. We were, in fact, discovering how tiring grief can be. Still, because it was on our way back to Minnesota, we decided to stop at Hannibal, Missouri, to see Mark Twain's boyhood home and spend the night. Mid-afternoon we checked into a motel not far from the restored historical part of town. We walked down to Cardiff Hill, past the white picket fence Tom Sawyer had whitewashed one summer—as I had done, I thought, the first summer we moved to Wyndmere. We toured the house where Twain had lived, the museum next door, and different buildings associated with Becky Thatcher and Huckleberry Finn. The boys insisted upon also going into a nearby "House of Horror." After I had paid the exorbitant entrance fee, Daniel became so frightened that he began to cry. I had to run with him through the rest of the house as fast as the two of us could go. Later, for a change of pace, we took a train ride out to a bluff overlooking the Mississippi, another spectacular view on a sunny afternoon. But by this time, even the train ride was wearing on our nerves. When I told the boys to smile for a picture, they stared at me with loathing and disgust.

We returned to the motel, and John and JoAnne decided to take a quick swim before supper. Daniel settled in to watch cartoons while I read. It was August 3, Daniel's seventh birthday. At one point I looked up from my book and found him in tears. John and he had both cried at other times on the trip, usually about bedtime, and once Daniel had said to JoAnne and me, "I want to die and be with Grandpa." Now, as I went over to find out what was going on and to hold him, Daniel asked me, "Dad, what does it mean to be heartbroken?"

I thought a moment. "It's when you feel so bad about something that you ache inside."

"That's how I feel about Grandpa," he said, as I picked him up.

"Me too, Dan. It's hard to believe he's gone."

My youngest son began to cry again. "It's not fair," he sobbed. "Grandpa promised to be at my birthday party, and now he won't be."

"I know that you're disappointed, Dan," I tried to reassure him, "but Grandpa will be there. Even if we can't see him, he'll be there."

I got another tissue and let my son blow his nose and wipe away his tears. "You've got Grandpa's eyes," I said. My son seemed pleased, even when I added, without thinking, "I didn't realize until Dad was dying that he had blue eyes."

Daniel moved over to give me a hug. "I love you, Dad," he said, "and I loved your dad."

"Thank you, Dan. I love you too." I held onto my youngest son.

"I will always be missing him, Dad."

"Me too, Dan. Always."

In the car the next day I recalled the words of C. S. Lewis in *A Grief Observed*: "My heart and my body are crying out, come back, come back." I realized that all of us who loved my father were experiencing this yearning to see him again.

A batch of letters and cards was waiting for us when we returned. Two from close friends, offered particular consolation. One was from Clayton, whom I had known for over twenty years, and with whom I had spoken briefly by phone before going on vacation:

> I have been thinking a great deal about you since hearing of your father's death. I am sure many people have offered their words of wisdom, support, and prayers. What can I offer? I'm sitting here trying to think of the right words, wanting, I guess, to take your grief away. Well, I can't; you know that. I can simply offer myself as a friend who shares your grief. I know the grace my father brought to me and without a doubt you must feel likewise about your father. The sequence of events is surely striking, and for some time to come, his death will pervade your waking and sleeping hours. I am glad you were there with him when he died. For each of you that moment embodies the essence of the life you shared and, with that, life can be more complete. Please extend my

love to JoAnne and the boys, as well as to your
mother. Our prayers of hope are with each of you.

And from Carrie, a former student, with whom I shared a
love of theology, literature, and Ireland:

I have thought of you so much since I heard
about your father's death. I cannot begin to understand the loss, grief, and the other range of emotions
that you are feeling and experiencing now. But I do
care, and I do wonder how you are. I remember the
story you told me once of the artist Andrew Wyeth
and the death of his father. Like him, have you been
feeling disconnected from everything? If so, do you
see the potential of "returning to self" up ahead; of
a revenant-like experience? I am wondering if some
of the grief you may be feeling is not only the loss of
a father that you have known for a lifetime, but also
the loss of the good relationship that you and he had
in more recent times? Kind of a double loss—both
old and new. Sometime I want to hear more how this
sad event has changed you, and where God and a
sense of eternity fit into it all, if they do.

Both letters touched me deeply. I was moved by their
compassion and that they had remembered me in this dark
hour of grief. I also felt as if they had somehow named precisely
what I had been experiencing: not only gratitude for being with
my father when he died, but the profound sense of loss,
knowing that Dad's and my relationship had finally reached
such a good point when he died. It was still too early, however,
to know how my father's death was changing me and where
God fit into all this.

CHAPTER VII

Into the Desert Places

> So great is the love between them and so
> strong the affection by which they are bound
> to one another and towards all the brethren
> that they are an example and a wonder to all.
> If anyone happens to want to live among
> them, as soon as they are aware of it, each of
> them offers him his own cell.
>
> —Rufinus

I SPENT THE WEEK AFTER OUR FAMILY vacation working furiously on the talk I was to give at Oxford University. Mom had insisted that I go to Ireland and England, and JoAnne gave me the distinct impression that it would somehow be good for me to be alone with my grief. So, despite continuing problems with my computer, I put the finishing touches on my writing. What I found in going back to my earlier work was how much my perspective on Cassian and the desert elders had changed since the death of my father. I also discovered how much my understanding of my father changed when I sat a while with the desert spiritual tradition that Cassian outlines in his writings.

I had initially been drawn to John Cassian not only because of his prominence in early Christianity, but because the desert spirituality he describes was so thoroughly incorporated into the life of the early Celtic Christians in Ireland and the British Isles. A leading church father who lived in the late fourth and early fifth centuries, Cassian is considered one of the most influential writers on the development of Christian spirituality in both East and West. His writings on the desert Christians have been read and appreciated by such spiritual leaders as Columban, Benedict, Gregory the Great, Alcuin, Dominic, Thomas Aquinas, Ignatius Loyola, Teresa of Avila, Francis de Sales, and John Henry Newman. A key idea in Cassian's theology is one that he learned directly from the desert holy men with whom he lived for some years in Egypt and Palestine. These desert Christians taught him that it is essential for everyone to speak directly from the heart to another person, and that this self-disclosure is good for the soul. They knew from experience what other spiritual traditions affirmed as a sound psychological and theological principle: If you are looking for a healer's cure, you must lay bare the wound.

In the desert, healing of spiritual diseases was done by confessing to the elders, wise men and women, mostly lay people, who listened with compassion and offered forgiveness and hope through their acceptance. According to Cassian, such a wise and experienced guide can be "the greatest gift and grace of the Holy Spirit." Besides the terms of *abba* for a male or *amma* for a female wisdom figure in the desert, the elder or spiritual guide was identified as a *pneumatikos pater* or *mater*: a spirit-bearer who acts as a kind of parent or midwife of souls. Desert Christians believed that a relationship of friendship with these guides could have a major effect on the direction of a person's spiritual journey, for, as they learned from the gospels, one person's spirit is very much affected for good or for ill by another's. They also taught that more might be learned from a person's example of Christian living than through any words he or she might preach; as they said, "a saintly life is more educative than a sermon."

Cassian's primary contribution was his insight that those who commit themselves to Christian living require the guidance of holy mentors, spiritual confessors, elders to whom can be disclosed "the counsels of the heart." To be close to an elder or to live with him or her for a while was necessary for spiritual growth and psychological maturity, and important for becoming an elder, spiritual guide, or mentor. This recognition of the value of an elder and of the practice of lay confession later spread to Ireland and other Celtic strongholds in Scotland, England, Wales, the Isle of Man, and Brittany. It contributed to the rise of the *anamchara* or soul-friend tradition, which in its creative origins included both female and male confessors, laypeople and ordained. I had researched this history for my doctoral dissertation at Notre Dame and had continued to write about it after becoming a professor of theology at the College of St. Catherine in St. Paul, Minnesota.

But something changed for me when I returned to my writing following the trip to Springfield, New Harmony, and Hannibal with my family. As summer lightning illuminates familiar landscape in a new, sometimes startling way, I suddenly saw that what Cassian learned in the desert was also what I was learning through the death of my father: that deeds speak more loudly than words. I, who loved books and respected words, now recognized that some people say "I love you" or "I'm sorry" through their actions and their deeds. My father was one of them. A man with the gift of listening well, he weighed his words carefully before speaking, and he consistently expressed his love nonverbally. I, who expected a verbal approach from him, possibly because my mother never seemed to lack for words, missed the numerous times he had been providing, through his actions, and yes, his tears, lessons in what he truly valued.

In those few days as I prepared to leave for Europe, I realized something more. By returning to the desert spirituality of Cassian, I came to see that my dad, like the desert elders, had functioned for his community in Wyndmere and the other places he lived as a lay spiritual guide, confessor, *abba*. Dad had the charism and personality that people trusted; they disclosed what was on their minds and, even more important, what was in their hearts. He listened to their stories and accepted them without judgment. They left feeling better about themselves, more hopeful, more capable of making needed changes.

I knew then that all those years behind the bar, Dad was doing what I had been studying about historically for almost two decades! It finally hit me that his ministry was what the desert fathers and Celtic Christians had been doing centuries earlier. It took his death for me to recognize that his was a truly ancient and honorable profession, and that he was the kind of father for whom I had always searched. This insight was exhilarating. It also became one more thong in a whip of regret that I used to beat myself. "Why?" I would ask myself repeatedly in Ireland and England. "Why did it take me so long to recognize the goodness of my father?"

Something that I discovered a year later, when I went back to revise my Oxford talk on Cassian for a journal publication, was that John Cassian's feast day is celebrated in the West on July 23, the same day my father died.

Carl Jung has a psychological term for such meaningful coincidences. He describes the convergence of seemingly unrelated phenomena and events in a meaningful way as "synchronicity." Theologians, Christians, have other words, such as "providence" or "grace." None of these words or views, of course, explains why things happen as they do. I have learned, however, always to pay attention to the experience of things inexplicably coming together, believing that the mystery of God is somehow revealed in and through them. Throughout the two weeks I spent in Ireland and England, I was to experience a great deal of synchronicity, which I identified with God's grace and my father's help. From the start of that journey abroad, I had a profound sense that Dad was accompanying me, leading me to the right people and to the right places—not only for my research, but for my peace of soul.

Before I had any inkling, though, of what I might find on my European sojourn, I phoned my mother in Kensal. I wanted to tell her good-bye before I left for Ireland, my first stop, and to ask her one more time if she was supportive of my going.

"Mom," I said, "are you sure that you'll be all right? I won't go if you don't think I should."

"No," she reassured me, "you should go. I'll be fine. I have a lot to do right now, and I can always call Marybeth or Dale or the relatives if I need any help."

"Well, I'll come and spend a week with you in Kensal when I get back," I promised. "Then I can help you sort Dad's clothes and answer the cards and letters of condolence."

"That would be great. But don't worry about me. Just go. Dad would want you to."

I flew into Ireland August 9, landing at Dublin airport in the early afternoon. Once I'd retrieved my luggage, I took a bus into the city. I had been to Ireland on numerous occasions before this trip, including the autumn of 1988 when, besides staying in Oxford at St. Theosevia's, I had taught a course in spirituality at Maynooth, outside of Dublin. This time, at work on a book about the Celtic saints, I intended to consult with certain scholars in the country, and, with a rented car, to go to some of the sites connected with particular Irish saints. Something I had learned over the years was that I could write much more vividly about the past by actually visiting those places that held collective memories. Despite the growth of towns and cities throughout Ireland over the centuries, however, many of the sites with their monastic ruins were still isolated, some not even appearing on any modern maps. In imitation of the desert Christians whose lives and sayings they had read, the early Celtic saints had built their monasteries in secluded mountain areas, forest glens, and on islands off the coast. They sometimes even used the word *dysert*, meaning "desert," to name certain solitary places, such as Dysert O'Dea (Desert of God), in order to show their affection for the earlier desert elders and their commitment to an ascetic lifestyle.

Still very tired, since I had not slept on the plane, I spent my first morning in Dublin checking in at a hotel down from the famous Post Office on O'Connell Street, where the Irish rebels held out against British troops during the Easter Rising of 1916. Following a "Plowman's Lunch" of assorted cheeses and brown bread at the hotel, I set out for the National

Museum to see, once again, the artifacts and relics on display from the Early Irish Church. Because of my continuing research into that historical period, each time I went to the museum I discovered more with which I was familiar. Even what I had recognized and appreciated on earlier trips, such as the Ardagh Chalice, Lismore Crosier, Tara Brooch, Cross of Cong, and St. Patrick's Bell Shrine, amazed me with their beauty and delicate craftsmanship. Later in the afternoon, on another sweep through antiquarian bookshops, I came across a copy of a book by Nora Chadwick on the Celtic saints. I couldn't believe my eyes! It was a classic and had been out of print for years. I had been trying to find it in the United States and on previous visits to Ireland, Scotland, and Wales. Just when I had given up on ever finding it, there it was on the shelf, waiting for me! I was astonished and grateful, and I whispered under my breath as I held it in my hands, "Thank you, Dad."

The next morning, after a dinner the night before with Father Diarmuid O'Laoghaire, a Jesuit scholar and friend, I rented a car and drove to Ferns, the home of Maedoc, one of my favorite Celtic saints. Nicknamed Son of the Star, Maedoc was a sixth-century holy man who, according to the early legends, was a protector of wildlife, including stags and wolves. I got out of my car and quickly toured the grounds where only a stone church now stands, hoping to get a sense of the place as it once was. The few castle remains from a later era than the saint's were not helpful. But the story of two Irish soul friends' love for each other and their separation lived on. In my imagination I looked for the trees that are described in one of the early medieval hagiographies. As the story goes,

> Maedoc and Molaise of Devenish were comrades who loved each other very much. One day they sat praying at the foot of two trees. "Ah, Jesus," they cried, "is it your will that we should part or that we should remain together until we die?" Then one of the two trees fell to the south, and the other to the north. "By the fall of the trees," they said, "it is clear

that we must part." Then they told each other good-
bye and kissed each other affectionately. Maedoc
went to the south and built a noble monastery at
Ferns in the center of Leinster, and Molaise went
north to Lough Erne and built a fair monastery at
Devenish.

This story reminded me, of course, of my father, and of a
separation even more difficult to bear than when two friends
decide to travel to two different geographical locations. Still,
between the lines, I recognized a certain truth: even such
separations, as painful as they are, may bear fruit, may become
something so much richer than the soul friends could imagine
at the time they are painfully following what they perceive to
be God's will. Perhaps, I thought, there is something more that
I am receiving—and that God is giving—in the midst of this
horrible sense of Dad's absence. The story, at least, seemed to
say that despite separations, whenever or however they come,
soul friendship itself endures.

I got back in my car and drove on to Ardmore, a small town
perched directly on the southern coast. By the time I arrived
there in late afternoon, the bright sunshine of the morning had
changed to fog and a fine mist. Checking in at the Cliffside
Hotel, I set out on foot to see the town's famous twelfth-century
round tower and the ruins where St. Declan, an early saint who
organized Christianity in Ireland before Patrick arrived,
founded a religious community. I had previously read in a Life
of St. Declan, written in the tenth century, that the monastery
he had built was "illustrious and beautiful," and that many
people were drawn to it "by the fame of his holy living," and,
as a result, "devoted themselves, soul and body, to God." As I
climbed the hill with the round tower barely visible through
the white mists, I came upon a cemetery near the ruins of the
cathedral church. On a recent grave a bouquet of flowers with
a black ribbon and the words "We Miss You, Grandpa" caught
my eye. Another small block of black marble with the inscrip-
tion "For Grandpa, Love Jonathan" brought back the recent

funeral in my own family. I lingered for a while, moved by the numerous tombstones and monuments shrouded in the dim light. A lone statue of a white angel stood upon one of the tombstones with its arms pointing toward the church.

I stumbled off in that direction, passing other ghostly pilgrims who had also come there to view the monastic ruins or to visit the graves of loved ones. I took several pictures of the panel carvings on the side of the medieval cathedral. These bas-reliefs on the west gable portrayed in stone certain stories from the scriptures, beginning with the scene of Adam and Eve in the Garden; they contained stories from the period of the early Celtic saints too. While I appreciated their charm as well as the grandeur of the round tower standing almost one hundred feet high, its conical top hidden in the mist, I was really in search of Declan's hermitage. According to the ancient hagiography, he had constructed it overlooking the ocean "in a narrow place at the brink of the sea." He had done so for his own "soul-making," realizing that "his last days were at hand," so that, in preparation for his death, he might be able "to read and pray and fast there."

I left the hill and walked through the town, past the hotel where I had registered. Farther along the coast on the same strip of road, I at last came upon Declan's holy well and what was left of his hermitage. Stopping for a moment, I prayed for my parents in front of the small carved crosses perched on a stone slab above the well. Then I followed the path toward the end of the heather-covered cliffs. A strong wind blew the wild white daisies and yellow gorse that were growing near the dirt trail and picked the seagulls up in midair, throwing them off-balance in their flight. I followed the path along a great stretch of rough wild grass and uncultivated heathland that led to the cliffs, and then, at the end, I could see the ocean on all sides of the promontory. As I reached the farthest point and looked out over the waters of the bay, the thick fog began to lift and the sun appeared behind the receding clouds. I noticed other seagulls circling a fisherman's boat in Ardmore harbor, wheeling and crying above the surface, diving now and again in search of food, their grayish-white feathers glistening with salt spray. They were waiting to be fed from the leftover scraps that would soon be tossed overboard. "You know your friends," I said half-aloud to them as they circled, recalling the hundreds of birds that showed up at Dad's burial.

As I stood there, at the edge of the cliffs, looking out over the ocean depths with the copper and crimson rays of the setting sun reflected in the waters, I was awed by the natural beauty of the place and the power of winds and tides. I began to weep uncontrollably, a grief that rose from deep within me that could not be contained. "Dad, Dad, I miss you," I cried. "I want you back again." It was my first experience in Ireland of keening, of crying from the heart for those we miss and love. It was not my last. I would be overcome with the onrush of tears numerous times on this pilgrimage to the land of the Celtic saints, the home of my spiritual ancestors, with my father as my companion and guide.

The next day, a Sunday, I drove into Cork and participated in a Eucharist at the Anglican cathedral of St. Findbarr. I had thought it was Roman Catholic, but by the time I found it, the bells were ringing and the service was about to start. I appreciated the welcome I received as a stranger and decided to stay. A father and his two sons made room for me in the pew. One of them reminded me of my son John; he handed me a hymnal. After the service I spoke outside briefly with the Anglican bishop who had presided. An older man with white hair who looked very much like a scholar with his glasses perched on the end of his nose, he responded immediately when I told him that I was working on a book about the Irish saints, including Findbarr. "Findbarr was a great teacher," the bishop told me. "As you probably know from your research, he was led to Cork by an angel who said to him, 'Stay here! This will be your place of resurrection.'"

"Yes," I told him, "I remember that Cork is the site of the school Findbarr started. It eventually produced a large number of Ireland's spiritual leaders. But wasn't he considered a great healer too?"

"Right," the bishop replied, obviously enthused that he had found someone else who was interested in his favorite saint. "There are all sorts of stories about Findbarr's healing ability. The earliest ones tell of how oil, a symbol of healing, poured out of the earth where Findbarr planted a cross when he got to Cork. Oil is said to have risen up over his sandals and over the sandals of the elders who were with him—an oil that healed every ailment."

"What I remember especially about him," I said, "is the story of his being without a soul friend." I knew this legend well, since I had used it in a book that I'd written on mentoring.

"I don't know that one," the bishop responded, looking perplexed. "Tell it to me."

"Well, according to an ancient hagiography, Findbarr's soul friend dies suddenly, and he goes to look for someone to take his place. He travels to another monastery and meets the abbot Eolang. Before Findbarr can ask the abbot about being his new soul friend, the latter kneels before him and says, 'I offer to you, Findbarr, my church, my heart, and my soul.' Findbarr is so overcome by the man's generosity, that he begins to weep. 'It was my thought that I'd be the one to offer my church, my heart, my soul to you.' Then the two men become lifelong soul friends." I paused a moment, reflecting on the power of the story, and added, "You know, it's really about how God sends soul friends into our lives when we most need them, sometimes at the most unexpected times."

The bishop, who had been listening intently, smiled appreciatively and nodded his agreement. He then gave me directions to Gougane Barra, the island retreat where in the seventh century Findbarr, like St. Declan at Ardmore, had built a hermitage and sought solitude in his last days. It was a beautiful, sunny day when I began my drive through the lush, green Irish countryside. While I drove, my conversation with the bishop kept coming back to me. I prayed to Findbarr for healing, and to God in gratitude for the soul friends that had come into my life, often when I needed them most.

As I approached Gougane Barra, once a desert place for Findbarr, but now a popular destination for modern pilgrims, I passed buses and cars loaded with the children, adolescents, the elderly, entire families. "Findbarr definitely wouldn't have found much quiet here," I thought, "if he were still alive!" I stopped and picked up three young male hitchhikers holding handmade signs with "Gougane Barra" printed on them. Once they had settled in my car, they wanted to know all about music in the States and to discuss the latest movies. When we had reached the place where buses and cars were parked, they went their way, more interested, it seemed, in the numbers of young women than in any retreat site, no matter how holy. A sobering thought occurred to me as I watched them walk away, "It won't be long and my sons will be their age."

Despite the crowds of people at Gougane Barra, I loved the place. Just off the shore of the lake, which is the source of the River Lee, I could see a small island about half an acre in size on which had been built a small, gray stone chapel. Surrounded by brooding cliffs and mountain peaks, shining brightly in the summer sun, this island is connected to the mainland by a short causeway. I walked across and entered the chapel. Other pilgrims were lighting candles, kneeling quietly in prayer, or chasing small children down the aisles. I knelt too, and as I prayed, noticed the stained-glass windows with images of familiar Irish saints, such as Findbarr, Patrick, Brendan, and Brigit. I lit a candle for my father and my mother and left the church. I followed a group of students to a large courtyard, located just behind the chapel. A tall, wooden cross was set in the middle of it. In the days of the Early Celtic Church, this hermit's cross showed people that this was the home of a dedicated person who valued solitude. I stayed there for a short time, watching modern pilgrims come and go, taking pictures of the site. It was a pleasant afternoon, and I would have remained longer, but I wanted to reach Kinsale, my next destination, that evening.

On my way from Gougane Barra through the mountains and onto a coastal road, I noticed a sign, "To Hare Island." It took a few moments for it to register that this must be the same island that I had read about in another hagiography, the place where St. Ciaran had once lived briefly before founding his monastery in the middle of Ireland at Clonmacnois. I remembered that an early legend told of a time when the holy man was escaping hostile brethren who sought to do him harm. Like other Celtic saints, Ciaran lived close to nature and counted many wild animals as his friends. So, as he prepared to leave, he put his books on a wild stag, one that used to accompany him wherever he went. This stag led Ciaran to Hare Island, where he decided to live for a while. Again, as frequently happened to both desert elders and Celtic saints, people would not leave him alone. Even a bishop from Britain came to see him, seeking guidance. Probably not appreciating the interruption of his solitude, Ciaran still received the bishop hospitably. But the devil encouraged the bishop to envy Ciaran's holiness. Ciaran, aware that envy is usually a result of unhappiness with one's own state in life, gave the bishop a gift of great value, a fine chalice with three carved golden birds, a symbol of the Trinity. The bishop, the story goes, was awestruck by Ciaran's generosity and repented immediately of his sin, kneeling before the holy man and asking his forgiveness. Ciaran gave it freely.

Remembering the story, I pulled my car over to the side of the road, and turned back to follow the sign to Hare Island. I had no idea how far the island might be, and was a bit anxious, knowing that in Ireland one might go for hours without seeing anything posted that resembled directions. Finally, after about an hour of driving, I stopped at a pub that I had passed earlier. Except for an occasional farmhouse, there were no other buildings in that part of the countryside. Inside the pub, through clouds of smoke, I detected a few customers, playing cards. Behind the bar was a tall, heavyset man who appeared to be the owner. The entire scene took me back to Wyndmere and to Ed's Bar and Lounge, and I thought to myself, "Ah, another slow afternoon for this poor guy!" Despite the lack of business, the bartender was friendly, and did not seem to mind my question about Hare Island.

"It's just over the next hill," he assured me. Walking out the door with me, he pointed, "Stay on that road."

I thanked him for his assistance but couldn't help muttering under my breath, "I've heard that before." I drove for twenty minutes. Then the road got increasingly narrow. Suddenly, I slammed on my brakes. My car had come to the end of a pier!

I had passed some children on the way to the pier, and two women who turned out to be their mothers. One of them came up to the car as I sat there, cursing quietly and wondering what to do next. "You're not going to be able to go any further," she said smiling, "at least in that."

I gritted my teeth and smiled back, "I was looking for Hare Island."

"That's it," she said, pointing to an island, off in the distance, with its grassy shores barely visible. "You won't be able to get there today though. The boat isn't running."

I explained to her why I was looking for the island and of my interest in the saints. "Come on in," she said, "and have tea with us. My name is Jill, and my husband, Tom, is a Methodist minister. Two friends who are visiting us are in the ministry, too."

I spent a good hour with all of them, enjoying a conversation that covered a wide spectrum of Irish political and religious topics. They were intrigued by my research and especially wanted to know more about the leadership of the women saints in the Celtic churches. Over scones, jam, and tea, I told them about St. Brigit, who lived at Kildare in the sixth century, and how the legends said that she had been ordained a bishop. There was also St. Ita of Killeedy, who heard confessions and forgave sins, and the holy abbess Samthann, who had a crosier, a bishop's staff, in her possession that worked miracles. One of the best stories was about St. Canair, a woman who was buried on Scattery Island, not too far away. She had once challenged an older male saint who didn't want her settling there by telling him, "Christ came to redeem women no less than men. He suffered for the sake of women as much as for the sake of men. Women too can enter the heavenly kingdom. Why, then, should you not allow women to live on this island?" The holy man, St. Senan, was so surprised by her challenge—and her theology!— that he allowed her to stay.

As I prepared to leave, the other couple offered to show me the route back. I thanked my hosts for their hospitality and then followed David and Elizabeth's car until it came to the road to Kinsale, a large town in southern Ireland near the mouth of the Bandon River, not far from the coast.

It was dusk when I reached the outskirts of town. After waving a thank you to my guides as they drove off, I sought directions to the Carmelite Friary where Father Peter O'Dwyer, a scholar I had met on other trips, was spending the summer. He had not been well but had suggested in a letter that I drop by for a talk about my research. I had first contacted him when I was teaching at Maynooth, and he, like Father O'Laoghaire, had mentored me when I needed advice and encouragement. Peter, a man in his sixties, had written about the Celi De, an early medieval reform movement in the Celtic churches that had been inspired by the ascetic practices and stories of the desert Christians. These Celi De, or Companions of God, valued highly the spiritual heritage of their own peoples; they combined the desert Christians' appreciation of solitude and simplicity with their own love of nature, learning, and the communion of saints.

I found the friary and was greeted at the door by a young monk. When Peter came into the foyer where I waited, I noticed immediately that he seemed to have aged a great deal since we had last met. Although I knew of his illness, I was not prepared for his whitened hair and the signs of strain around his eyes. He moved slowly as he led me to another room where we could sit more comfortably. We sat across from each other, and as we talked, the last rays of the sun faded through the window. It became more difficult to see his face. My distinct impression was of a wise and holy man sitting there, attentive to our conversation, dressed in the long brown robes and cowl of a friar. When he walked with me back to my car an hour later, his eyes filled with tears when I told him my dad had just died.

"Would you pray for him, please?" I asked him.

He nodded his head and replied, "And I'll pray for you too." Then he added words that were prophetic, "It will take a long time to get through this kind of grief, and it will be especially hard when your travelling is over." His tears took me back to another time when I was telling my father good-bye as I left for the seminary.

That night I remembered that it had been three years ago that very day that John, Daniel, and I had set out on our journey to North Dakota and then, with Dad and Mom, on to Mendora and the Black Hills. I prayed in gratitude for the insights that had come from that trip, the "pricking of the boil," as it were, that helped me eventually heal my relationship with my father before he died. I thanked the Holy One, too, for the love of my parents and all that they had given me; for my wife and the new harmony her love had brought into my life; for my children that they would grow strong in their Christian faith. I also prayed for the kind strangers and the friendly scholar who had offered me hospitality that day, and who, like Ciaran with his gift to the envious bishop, assured me, without knowing, that I was still lovable, still capable of being forgiven.

I left the farmhouse bed-and-breakfast early the next morning, wanting to get a good start on the day. It was one that I had anticipated for years. I planned actually to set foot on Skellig Michael, a rugged island off the western coast of Ireland that housed one of the most ancient surviving sites of the Early Celtic Church. The sky was filled with a bright sun and billowy white clouds as I drove onto the Ring of Kerry, reassuring me. I knew that Skellig Michael was only accessible during mild weather and the summer months, and that if I didn't make it out that day, I would probably miss my chance for some time to come. Every time I saw an advertisement along the road about boats going out to the skellig rocks, I stopped to ask the times they might go and the cost. As the morning progressed, however, I became increasingly more anxious. Everywhere I inquired the boats were either already filled or not in service. Discouraged and tired from my frantic pace, I finally pulled into Ballinskelligs, a small seaport town on the Ring of Kerry, and rented a room at a comfortable bed-and-breakfast not far from the shore.

It was mid-afternoon and, after storing my luggage in an upstairs room, I decided to take a walk on the beach. Without thinking, I put an extra roll of film in my pocket and set out with my camera in hand. By this time I was feeling slightly depressed, especially when I noticed that the posted signs said that no boat trips were scheduled for the following day. "Once again," I thought to myself, "I will have to be content with staring at the island from the shore as I have done on previous trips." As I reached the dock, however, I noticed a boat about to leave. "Hey," I yelled, "where are you going?"

I heard a voice shout back from someone who appeared to be the captain, "Out to Skellig. Come on, we have room for one more."

I couldn't believe my ears! I jumped aboard, thrilled at the opportunity to visit at last the holy site I had been longing to see firsthand.

Skellig Michael, like many of the high places in Celtic lands, is named after the archangel St. Michael, for whom the early Christians had special reverence. I prayed almost constantly to him as our tiny boat with twenty passengers sailed across a choppy sea. We were sometimes caught up in the angry waves,

our boat floundering momentarily, before being set down on
the surface of the water and then drenched by the swells of the
sea. It took the skipper almost forty minutes before he had
pulled the boat alongside the wooden pier on a side of the
island that, by comparison with the other sides, was relatively
calm. While he tied the boat to a sturdy post and tried to hold
it fast, we took turns jumping to the bank. That was the easy
part. We had yet to climb at a fast pace another twenty minutes
or more up the sides of Skellig Michael to where the monastic
ruins were located.

I thought I was in fairly good shape, but by the time I
reached the ridge where the ruins were visible, I was physically exhausted and winded. At the same time I was thrilled
to be there and invigorated. While other monastic sites
scattered throughout Ireland and the British Isles contain
little except rocks and ruins, usually from the later medieval
period, there before me were the beehive-shaped cells, stone
oratory, and carved crosses of one of the earliest settlements
of the Irish church. Still in almost perfect shape, they remain
fairly untouched by the ravages of wind, rain, and time. As I
stood there catching my breath, the boat trip out in the
bright rays of the afternoon sun and my climb to the rugged
heights of this remote island seemed like the culmination of
a lifelong quest. For over a decade and a half, since I had
first heard the word *anamchara,* Gaelic for "soul friend," I
had been intrigued, literally haunted, by that spiritual
heritage. Now, at last, I could actually see and touch the cells
and oratory where the early Irish monks had once lived and
prayed, imitating in their isolation and meager sustenance
the desert elders whom they loved.

The bee-hive huts themselves had become for me a fitting
symbol of soul-friendship. Among the desert Christians, cells
were considered quiet places where one opened one's heart to
God, a place to learn "everything." To share a cell with another
was to share one's inmost self, one's mind, and heart. The
emergence of soul-friendship in Ireland, especially among the

Celi De, was a natural development from the desert, and like the desert guides, an *anamchara* was originally a companion with whom one shared a cell and to whom one confessed. Those Irish Christians believed that such a friendship has bonds that can never be broken—not even by death. They were familiar with the words of John Cassian: "There is one kind of love which is indissoluble, what no interval of time or space can sever or destroy, and what even death itself cannot part. With God the union of character, not of place, joins friends together in a common dwelling."

I entered one of the six bee-hive cells, stooping to get in because of the low doorway. The inside walls were of rock, so closely fitted together that rain could not penetrate. Considering the space, perhaps only two or three monks could live inside. The room itself, I thought, would not be considered luxurious by any standards. The monks probably built a fire in the middle of the room for cooking, and surely for warmth during the cold winter months. Because of the cramped conditions, it would be difficult to stretch out at all to sleep. There were no windows to let light in. In such an extremely ascetic existence, a person must have come to value highly human companionship and friendship. Even with others, I thought, a profound sense of solitude must have remained constant on Skellig Michael, with only the vast heavens above and the tides of the raging sea hitting the island continuously below.

I left the cell and walked a few steps over to the boat-shaped oratory. Again I had to stoop to enter, probably a good reminder to the monks, and to myself, to avoid the sin of pride. Both desert and Celtic Christians warned against that pretension of playing God—or not needing God in one's life. I sat quietly on the stone floor, trying to imagine the group of monks crawling in, as I had just done, and sitting down in the crowded space each morning and evening to offer prayers and hear the scriptures read. They, too, must have called to mind loved ones who had preceded them in death and, for support and guidance, upon the entire communion of saints. Prayer

would have come naturally to them, their lives so enmeshed in
nature, so closely-tied to the wind and the waves. What would
have brought them out to this island, I wondered, to live in
such harsh conditions? Was it not their own consciousness of
sin and human fragility, and their desire to place themselves
totally in God's hands—to submit their lives in a daily act of
surrender in hopes of being forgiven, of being saved?

I sat there, lost in thought and deep in prayer. When I
finally left the sacred precincts, mindful that the boat would
be leaving soon, I paused at the cemetery nearby. At the foot
of one of the stone crosses I placed a fragile, white flower that
I had picked on my climb up. It had been clinging to the rocks,
watered only by the damp air and lingering mist. Another story
came to me, this time about Oengus the Culdee, a ninth-cen-
tury saint, who left his hermitage cell in Munster and went in
search of Maelruain, one of the founders of the Celi De, who
became his soul friend. On the way, Oengus saw a grave in a
churchyard, perhaps the one still at Tallaght, outside of Dublin
where the Celi De had lived. In this story it was said to be
surrounded by multitudes of angels. Oengus asked the priest
of the church, "Who has been buried there?"

"A certain wretched man who lived in the place," the priest
replied.

"What good has he done?" said Oengus.

"Truly, we had a hard time seeing anything good that he
did," said the priest, "except for one thing: from morning to
nightfall, he recounted the deeds of the saints of the world."

"O God of heaven," Oengus exclaimed, "anyone who
makes a song of praise for the saints, great will be that
person's glory."

I remembered my father as I stood there by the stone cross
where the flower lay. I prayed in gratitude for him, recalling,
as I did, my own blindness, like that of the priest's in the story,
to the good that one man can accomplish.

I climbed farther up the rocks to get a better view of the entire enclosure and to take more pictures for my students back home. I had just reached the top of a bluff and looked down when I suddenly remembered my Thomas Merton dream of fifteen years before. In it he had pointed out to me what looked to be a series of rounded churches. There below me was my dream: the round bee-hive huts so closely intertwined, vividly expressing the contours of mandalas! I reflected upon this synchronicity, and the meaning it expressed. For years I had been studying the history of the Early Celtic Church and been impressed with how different it was from so much of contemporary Christianity. That Early Celtic Church valued small ecclesial communities whose members knew one another by name. It fostered greater mutuality and collaboration between ordained and lay leaders, because it knew from experience that everyone benefits when each person's gifts are welcomed hospitably. It took for granted that women would function in a great variety of leadership roles. It saw humanity, Mother Earth, and all of creation as intimately related. Above all, this church appreciated what I was coming to value even more since my father's death: family ties and friendships that last an eternity.

As I stared down at the bee-hive huts on that remote desert place off the coast of Ireland, I realized that this was my vision of church, of what I hoped that Christianity would someday become. My dream and this gift from the past shed light on the future, and on what I would spend my energies trying to bring about.

CHAPTER VIII

Grief Throughout the World

> So vast the grief, so universal through the world.
> —Alcuin

THAT EVENING, AT THE HUNTSMAN Restaurant in Waterville, off the coast of western Ireland where sky and sea merge into a union of clouds, water, and light, I celebrated alone this most memorable of days. A waitress had brought me a glass of scotch, which I sipped slowly as I awaited a dinner of fresh lobster caught in the bay that afternoon. I was feeling extremely grateful for finally having set foot on Skellig Michael, for the boat ride out, the bee-hive cells, the wind, the sea. Those rhythms of nature and memories of ancient religious history, I knew, had lived in my soul long before I was consciously aware, for decades, for centuries.

I sat there looking through the window toward the boats on the pier, caught up in recollections of the day and of my father. My thoughts, however, were interrupted by a nearby conversation. Judging from the tone and the volume of the voices, the American couple and their family had not had a good day. It was clear that the woman was unhappy with her husband. At one point, when one of the teen-age sons began to relate something about his girlfriend to the group, I heard his mother tell him, with derision in her voice, "Don't tell your father a thing." I found myself irritated by her bitter tone and advice, and I thought to myself, "What a thing to tell your son!" In effect she was saying, "Don't trust your father!" I realized, as I took another sip from my scotch, that here was one more example of the pull between "mother-love" and "father-love" that every child faces, most often unconsciously, a tug of loyalties that can be exacerbated by one or both parents.

Scenes from my childhood came to mind as I stared out at the boats on the shore and the silver shimmer of the sea, fragments of memories that took me back to my childhood. One of my earliest recollections is of standing next to my mother in a doorway of some house. I am about two-and-a-half or three years old, and my parents are arguing. Dad has come home having had one too many drinks, and I can tell from my mother's voice that she is upset. I hear my father raise his voice in his defense, as my mother continues to show her disapproval. Both are angry, and I have not heard that tone in their voices before, directed at each other. Not understanding, and afraid as I witness this battle of the titans, I cling to my mother. "Yes," I thought to myself as I sat at the restaurant table, "that may have been at the root of my closeness to Mom."

I had always had a warm relationship with my mother. I was her firstborn, after all, and the only child in our family until I was nine years old. "The best years of my life," I had once jokingly told my wife, and she, a firstborn too, had smiled and agreed. I remembered my mother reading to me at night while my father worked, holding me when I was afraid of the thunder and the lightning, teaching me about God and the saints with stories that caught my imagination. Unconsciously I began to equate mother-love with unconditional love, the sense that no matter what I did or said, I would still be loved by her. Because of that, I believed that she could be trusted and that I could confide in her.

From my study of psychology years later, I knew about what Freud and others describe as an Oedipus complex, named after the Greek king in a play by Sophocles who, without knowing, kills his father and marries his mother.

Although Freud interprets it primarily as a sickness when intimacy with the mother is extremely intense and prolonged, Jung has a more positive understanding of the bonding between mother and son. He speaks of a mother complex, not necessarily pathological, in which a male child grows up feeling closer to his mother, and, Jung says, is thus capable of friendships of great tenderness with both women and men. Such a child is more likely to become a gifted teacher, have a feeling for history, and cherish the values of the past; he may be more receptive to revelation, endowed with a wealth of religious feelings, and able to bring into reality what Jung calls the *ecclesia spiritualis* or spiritual community. Mother-love has its advantages.

Father-love can be more complex. At least, that is how I experienced it. It was a type of love that seemed not to be so freely given. I had to earn it. There were certain standards by which I was judged as acceptable—and thus lovable—or not. I grew to believe that I had to somehow conform to my father's wishes in order to gain his approval and his love. At some point I reacted to this unconsciously; by adolescence and young adulthood I had cut Dad off emotionally. Anger and hurt had taken on a life of their own, especially, I think, because they had never been acknowledged or expressed. They led to the unconscious desire to punish, to get even. That was what probably lay behind my violent words to him that day so many years ago, "I wish you weren't my father." Somewhere along the line—beyond our political disagreements—I had come to believe that he didn't really love me as I was, and therefore I wouldn't love him either! Again, I neither recognized this consciously nor was I aware of how much I wanted him to love me, how much I hungered for his acceptance, how much I yearned to have a relationship with him that was as easy and as close as my relationship with my mother.

It was not until graduate school at Notre Dame that I learned through dreams that I must begin to look again at my relationship with my father. Several of my teachers were encouraging me to take my dreams seriously, so I had begun to record those that I remembered. I was amazed by their vividness and their sometimes blunt messages. Besides the Merton dream, one of the first dreams I recorded was one of a funeral taking place, the funeral of my father. This dream was very similar to the one that preceded his actual death. In this earlier dream, eighteen years before his death, Dad's funeral is the next day at Notre Dame, and I am crying and saying, "It isn't fair! I was just getting to know him!"

As I discussed the contents of the dream with Fritz, my friend and spiritual guide, it became apparent that the dream's message was that my relationship with my father, for whatever reason, had been dead to me for some time. It was also telling me that from deep within I wanted something different, something more. My tears spoke of that. Fritz helped me explore my relationship with Dad and helped me see, as Jung says, that conflict in a relationship, especially if it is highly emotional, is not necessarily a sign of lack of love but of strong ties and genuine affection. Where there is fire or passion between people, there is both the potential for great woundedness and for the creation of light. Fritz helped me realize that in emotionally cutting myself off from my father, I had in effect cut off my own potential fatherhood. He also pointed out that I was bound to have trouble trusting a God who is called Father if I didn't trust my own dad. In becoming my spiritual mentor, Fritz gave me the courage to reestablish inner and exterior connections; he gave me the freedom to change, to claim who I was and who I was not! With his support and encouragement, I began to make an effort to get to know my father better.

What I had failed to recognize, I thought, as I got up from the table at the Huntsman Restaurant and went to pay my bill, was that my father had always loved me, but with a father's love. Behind what I had considered "conditions" was *love*. I remembered the picture that I had searched for when I returned home from his funeral, the picture of my being lifted up on my father's shoulders, and the smile of someone who truly wanted *me* in this world.

Yes, I thought, climbing into my rented car and driving back along the country road that skirted the ocean, Dad did get angry with me for certain things I did as a child. But behind that anger was a father's passion to instill in his children what he considered right and good. Although he was obviously disappointed that I was more of a bookworm than a jock when I was growing up, those feelings evidently changed as he got older. As a close friend of Dad's told me at the reception after my father's funeral, "Your dad loved you. He was proud of your achievements. He acted as though you could walk on water." I had not known that. For too long I was a kid trying to please him and thinking that nothing I accomplished would. Yes, he had frequently challenged me to do better, had suggested ways I might change my life, but that didn't mean he didn't love me. "I understand this all much more," I said to myself as I drove, "for now I have a father's love for my own two sons. I too find myself challenging them to do their best while, at the same time, trying to be supportive of them. I'm also trying to say to them, more often than I heard when I was a growing up, 'I'm sorry' and 'I love you.'"

I drove back toward Ballinskelligs and the bed-and-breakfast where I would stay the night. I was looking for the cemetery that I had passed that afternoon. It had caught my attention as I drove by, for I knew that it was located near the site where Celi De monks, fleeing from Skellig Michael at the time of the Vikings' raids, had settled. In the car, tired and feeling a bit woozy from the scotch, I began to cry again, remembering a scene that took place even before the one in which I am clinging to my mother while she is arguing with Dad. In this memory I am about two years old and am choking on a candy jawbreaker. There is the horrible sensation that I cannot breathe. I don't know what to do. Mom is screaming, and Dad scoops me up in his arms, holds me by my legs, and pounds my back with his fist. I am upside down, petrified, almost blacking out. Suddenly the candy pops out of my mouth and I can breathe again.

"My God!" I said to myself as I continued driving, realizing that my father had not only given me life through his love for my mother, but had quite literally saved my life with his quick thinking! If it hadn't been for him, I thought, I wouldn't be alive today, driving down a road in Ireland. In fact, if it hadn't been for him, I might not even have become a traveller who visits foreign lands so frequently. My father was the one, after all, who introduced me to the wider world, a world outside of books. He was the one who invited me, as I sat beside him in the Standard Oil truck, beyond the hearth, the home, the world of "mother." Through his many friendships, he also taught me that this wider world, despite its conflict, tragedy, and injustices, is a holy place, a place of mystery and of magic, a place where God dwells. Dad, one of my first mentors, helped me prepare for my immersion in this world and my wandering over it.

Through the windshield and my tears I saw the cemetery and church ruins on my left. I turned down the narrow dirt road, and after a short ride pulled up to the black wrought iron gates. They were locked tightly with a giant metal padlock. I had to walk down along the stone walls that encircled the cemetery to another part where I was able to climb over. I stood there staring. All around me were gray and brown headstones and tombs, some in great need of repair. All except the newest were encrusted with lichen and moss. Yellow gorse and wild multicolored fuchsias interrupted the bleak landscape. Straight ahead of me beyond the graves was another stone wall, bordering a beach and the ocean. I could see Skellig Michael off in the distance, enshrouded in mist, and a few fishermen in small boats out on the waters, casting their nets for one last try before sunset.

I wandered among the tombs in this land of the dead, transfixed by the variety of sizes, the diverse names that were sometimes barely legible, the dates of unknown people's births and deaths. There were monuments that went back centuries; others appeared to be brand-new. On some of the graves were bouquets of ugly plastic flowers of different colors. A few headstones had angels made out of plaster, marking the spot where babies or children were buried. Except for the thundering surf on the stones and sands of the seashore, the place was totally silent; a silence that belonged to another age, a stillness in the air older than I could imagine. In this mournful, haunted place, the words of the English monk Alcuin came to me, "So vast the grief, so universal through the world."

My head throbbed from the crying that I had already done in the car. I felt drained of energy. As I stood there, however, listening to the silence, something else came over me, hitting me like a giant wave. I realized for the first time that I was not alone in my grief; everyone in the world had experienced or soon would know the pain of loss. It was as if I saw—no, experienced!—a new aspect of reality there among the tombs. I discovered that this world *is* filled with sadness, and that there is truth in what the nuns had taught me years before: We do live in a "vale of tears." All creation is caught up in this universal pattern; all creation is crying out for its lost ones; everyone is united in this anguish. Each person deals with this loss in different ways. Some strike back in their hurt and attempt to inflict pain, adding to everyone's misery. Some try to escape it by becoming withdrawn, apathetic, depressed. Others attempt to anesthetize the pain with sexual promiscuity, pornography, alcohol, or drugs. But there is another way, I thought, as I watched the last red streaks of sunlight on the horizon. It is the way of compassion, the way that opens us up to the suffering of others and seeks to heal rather than hurt.

I moved to the edge of the cemetery and climbed up the stone walls bordering the beach. I stood there quietly, looking out at the skellig rocks and fishermen. No longer protected by the walls surrounding the cemetery, I now heard the wind howling and moaning with ferocity. Above the noise of the surf an owl hooted somewhere in the trees. Exhausted by my grieving, I could no longer hold back my tears. They came again, like a sudden summer shower. I looked out over the ocean's dark blue depths, now lit only by the full moon and the first stars. I cried into the roar of the wind and the tumultuous onrush of the waves. I cried for my father, my mother, my wife, my sons, for me. I cried for all those untold millions that day who were also attempting to deal with their loss. No more inflicting pain upon those I love, I vowed. No more bitter remarks and accusations!

I keened that evening, crying from the heart, recognizing that with the death of my father I was no longer a child. If I had been experiencing a woundedness in our relationship before Dad's death, his dying had brought about an even deeper psychic wounding. I felt as if I had been brought to the edges of the spiritual realm. This realm was no longer merely an intellectual concept. Now I lived on the threshold with one foot in this world and one foot in the next. My father, the person who was such an intimate part of my life, lived in this other realm. Such knowledge of the heart created in me a raw psychic pain that resulted in tears at unexpected moments.

That night, after I returned to Ballinskelligs, I seemed to have one dream after another. In an especially vivid one my son John is picked at an early age to be a star athlete for a national soccer team. My father is very proud of him—as am I.

The following day, August 13, I drove across the Dingle Peninsula, one of the more remote and primitive areas of Ireland. On this day, however, everyone and his uncle seemed to be on holiday, driving bumper-to-bumper on the same roads as I—and parking at the same scenic lookouts. Despite the traffic, the natural beauty of the place was spectacular. Along the coast I saw dozens of bee-hive cells as well as the remains of a prehistoric fort. In the afternoon, as rain and fog blanketed the area, I stopped at the site of the famous Gallerus Oratory, an eighth-century stone church that looks like an overturned boat. Considered one of the oldest surviving Christian buildings in Ireland, it reminded me of the one on Skellig Michael, although this one was better preserved. I drove on to Ardfert, where the medieval ruins of a church and monastery dedicated to St. Brendan are located. Archaeologists were at work at the site, so I could only look through a fence at the screened-off area and try to imagine what it had once looked like.

After a full day of driving and getting lost on the winding roads, I finally pulled into the driveway of a little white cottage a short distance from the ocean near Kerry Head. A sign out front in large, black letters, "B & B," had attracted my attention. I was desperate. Mrs. Casey, proprietor, critically looked me over when I rang the bell and, when I passed some test of acceptability, agreed to let me stay the night. Relieved to have a place to rest, I took a shower and a short nap, then drove into the nearby town to a pub that Mrs. Casey told me had "real Irish music." I was expecting traditional music played with fiddle, flute, uilleann pipes, and perhaps a harp. As it turned out, however, the band was small, consisting of four members, and only played waltzes and slow dances. I sat at a table, ordered a beer, and spent the evening watching and listening to the locals. By Irish standards I had arrived early, so I was able to choose a good spot. The townspeople drifted in a few at a time, bringing their entire families with them. Soon the place was filled with adults, children, grandparents—even babies no older than a couple weeks. I felt as if I were back in Wyndmere at Dad's bar on a Saturday night; he had music then, and everyone turned out. Here in Ireland couples, young and old, danced across the floor. Sometimes children were held in their arms. Sometimes women danced with women, laughing as they whirled. The pub was filled with unpretentious people enjoying a night out, escaping, at least momentarily, the conflicts and fears that they faced daily.

About eight o'clock in the evening, as the pub grew more crowded, an elderly man and his wife approached and asked if they could sit at my table. I told them that they were welcome to do so, and while the woman talked with family members at the next table, the man started a conversation with me. In some ways he reminded me of my grandfather, Grandpa John, with his grayish-white hair, the deep furrows in his forehead, and his gnarled, thick hands, obviously used to hard labor. He told me that he loved to dance, even at his age, and that he came here often to enjoy the music. He assumed that I was an American and asked how I was liking Ireland and whether I was on holiday.

At some point during our conversation I mentioned that my father had died just a few weeks before. The older man's face changed at once from a smile to a look of concern. Tears came to his eyes, and he clasped my hand, telling me, "You're a gentle man; your father must have been a good man to have raised you. I'm sorry for you that he's gone." I was struck by the man's compassion, by his own gentleness, and by his immediate sensitivity to my suffering and grief. I thanked him for it, and even though I had barely spent more than an hour with him at the pub, I felt as if I had known him a lifetime.

Back at Mrs. Casey's I wrote in my journal: "It was three weeks ago today that Dad died. It seems like an eternity, and yet like yesterday. Pain does not subside with time, it seems only to deepen. I love you, Dad; I miss you."

The next day I was on the road again, this time in search of Killeedy, the home of St. Ita, whom I had mentioned to the Methodist couple near Hare Island. A sixth-century abbess in the Early Celtic Church, Ita was one of Ireland's greatest soul friends. She is portrayed in her hagiography as a confessor not only to her charges in the monastery, but to the laypeople who came to her to confess their sins. One story, in particular, told of a layman who had confessed murdering a person. Ita had him do penance for the sin he had committed, as well as to heal the inner wound of regret he carried. She had told him, "If you follow my advice, you will have eternal life." The story highlighted the importance of lay women confessors in the Early Celtic Church. It also affirmed, as do the Twelve Steps of Alcoholics Anonymous today, that, along with the human need to confess sins and wrongs, and thus take responsibility for our lives, we also need to make amends for the damage our sinful or wrong actions have caused.

St. Brendan the Navigator was one of the many foster sons Ita educated. He once asked her, according to an early legend, what the three works most pleasing to God were. Ita replied, "The three things that please God most are true faith in God with a pure heart, a simple life with a grateful spirit, and generosity inspired by charity." In the stories about Ita and Brendan found in the hagiographies, I especially appreciated certain references that shed light on the nature of soul friendships. Brendan, for example, smiled warmly, we are told, when he would think of Ita. Ita, in turn, is said to have experienced the slow passage of time when Brendan was away.

I was not smiling, however, when I turned off a road outside of Abbeyfeale to ask directions to Killeedy. I was desperate. The site of Ita's monastery did not appear on any map, and although I knew I was close, I didn't know precisely where it might be. "If anyone can help me," I thought, "it will be a nun." My intuitions proved accurate. The school I stopped at was deserted, with the children away on break, but as I walked the empty halls, I came upon a woman dressed in modern religious garb. Small in stature, she was obviously startled to see me. When I explained who I was and what I was looking for, she shook hands. "I'm Sister Eucharia," she said, smiling. "Come with me."

I followed her out of the school and into the nearby convent where she left me standing in the guest parlor as she went off to prepare hot tea. "Here, drink this," she said, upon her return, and motioned me to sit down. "You know, Ita is one of my favorite saints, and there's not much written about her. She's called the foster mother of the saints of Ireland—because of all the leaders she educated."

"Yes, I know," I replied, settling into one of the highly ornate stuffed chairs. "The research I'm doing shows what a spiritual leader she was in her own right. I'm intrigued by the stories that speak of her receiving guidance from her dreams. She was also known for her wisdom and generosity. By the way," I lifted the cup of tea to salute her, "thank you for your own."

"Don't mention it," Sister Eucharia replied. "Now, tell me, how can I help you?"

"Well, do you happen to know where Killeedy is? I've been searching all over, as I told you, and have had no luck."

"You've come to the right place!" she said, smiling once again. "It's not far from here."

"Thank God!" I said, relieved to know that I was at least somewhere in the vicinity. "Then, again," I thought to myself, "I've heard that line before." She seemed to recognize my apprehension.

"Really, it's quite near, about a half-hour from here," Sister Eucharia assured me, laughing outright. "I'll draw you a map."

For the first time in my numerous travels to Celtic lands, I found someone who gave accurate information. Twenty-five minutes after I had thanked Sister for her hospitality, and, most of all the handdrawn map, I arrived at what was left of Killeedy. Not much remained, except a lone sign, badly in need of fresh paint, and the stark, decaying walls of a late medieval church, surrounded on all sides by graves. Tall grass covered most of the area; near the church I could see a tall, ugly plaster statue of St. Ita, dressed as a nun in very traditional garb. "So, this is what's left of the place," I muttered as I got of the car. Then, hearing the noise of someone shoveling dirt, I glanced over to my left. There, in the midst of the graves, I could see a man digging. Dressed in a dark pants and a light, summer shirt, open at the collar, he appeared to be about fifty-five years old. I walked over to him, introduced myself, and asked if he knew where the holy well of St. Ita might be.

"Oh, it's right there," he said, pointing in the direction of the church. "It's hard to find because of the tall grass. I'll show you."

He led me to a small spring, covered over with grass and leaves, almost invisible to the human eye. It had once been a place where women bathed their children as a prevention against small pox. I took some pictures and, since the man seemed friendly and willing to talk, struck up a conversation with him.

"My name's Sean," he told me. "I come out here every now and then to take care of my uncles' graves. They were fine men, and I haven't forgotten their kindness to me when they were alive. This is the least I can do to show my appreciation."

I admired his devotion and told him what I did for a living.

"Have you never been here before?" Sean asked.

"No," I said, "this is my first time."

"Then, you must let me take you up into the hill country so that you can see all of Ita's valley spread out below you. I also can show you the site where Irish Catholics used to meet secretly during the days of the Penal Laws to hear Mass. Come on!"

Again, I was impressed that afternoon with another stranger's hospitality. Sean drove me up winding, muddy roads to a spot with a wonderful view. As far as the eye could see were lush fields of green, interrupted only by colors of brown and white where distant cattle and sheep grazed. Not far from where we parked, three men in overalls were painting a stone altar. Sean introduced me to them and explained that each year on a feast day in late August people would come out to this spot for Mass—to commemorate when their ancestors gathered there to pray at a time the Catholic faith was outlawed. "If they were caught," Sean told me, "they could lose their lives."

Later that evening, at the farmhouse where I was staying for the night, I remembered Sean's words about his ancestors and the tone of admiration in his voice for their bravery. What I admired about Sean, I thought, as I pushed back the covers and climbed into bed, was his respect for the past and his belief that the living are still very much connected with the dead. I was grateful for his hospitality to me but even more for the memory of him kneeling in the dirt, planting flowers at his uncles' graves.

The following day was as full and rich as the preceding ones. In the morning I left the farmhouse which had been my bed-and-breakfast. I had slept well, with cattle just outside my bedroom window munching quietly, reminding me of visits as a child to my grandparents' farm outside of Kensal. I drove like mad to get to Galway, the largest city on the western coast, where I spent a short time at Kenny's Bookstore, a place that had sent me over the years many books not available in the States. I wanted to stay much longer, wandering its hallowed halls and looking for illusive, out-of-print books. I was intent, however, upon reaching St. Patrick's College at Maynooth by nightfall. Before getting there, I intended to visit one more site which, like Killeedy, did not appear on any modern map.

I stopped numerous times that afternoon to inquire where Durrow might be located. Finally, a woman at a Tourist Information center in Ossory was able to give me directions to what was once a great monastery, founded by the priest-scholar-poet St. Columcille, a favorite saint of mine. His contemporaries considered him an exceptional teacher and healer. Like the desert elders, Columcille is portrayed in early hagiographies as a man who had fought evil spirits and "the furious rage of wild beasts." Despite his struggles, or perhaps precisely because of them, a sixth-century poem lauded him as "a gentle sage" and stated that "a priest was but one of his callings." I especially identified with the description that said he "never could spend the space of even one hour without study, prayer, or writing." Columcille founded many monasteries, two of which I had already visited on other trips: Kells, in Ireland, where the beautifully illuminated Book of Kells is said to have been finished; and Iona, a tiny island in the Hebrides off the western coast of Scotland, where he had gone as a missionary. Durrow was another monastic site associated with the saint.

I had wanted to visit Durrow since I had first seen the Book of Durrow on display, along with the Book of Kells, at Trinity

College in Dublin. It is one of the earliest illuminated books that has survived, and its primitive gospel figures, sketched in soft colors of red, yellow, brown, and green, evoked a response from deep within me, a yearning for the distant past and its spirituality. Now, as I pulled up before the gates of a private park, I remembered another story of Columcille. He had just built his church at Durrow when someone brought him bitter-tasting apples as a gift. He is said to have blessed them, and with his blessing, they became "quite sweet." I wondered about the meaning of that story.

I got out of my car and began walking down a long and winding path. I met a young father with two daughters headed in the opposite direction, on their way back to their car. They smiled at me when I greeted them and kept walking. I was looking for any signs of ruins that might have survived, and specifically for a high cross that was supposed to be one of the best still standing. I hurried, for I could tell that an afternoon rain shower was on its way. All that loomed ahead of me, however, was an old deserted Anglican church. Judging from its architecture, it had been built during the Victorian era. A cemetery, with many tombstones, surrounded it.

I walked around the grounds, aware that there was no one else there. Dark clouds covered the sky, and shadows deepened near the church and graves. The entire area began to remind me of a scene from the movie "Dracula," and I grew nervous and apprehensive. The trees in the grove bordering the cemetery had thick trunks, overgrown with ivy, and their leaves rustled in the summer wind. The shutters on the broken windows of the church rattled ominously.

Then, in the midst of all this gloom, I saw the tall stone cross with its scenes from the scriptures and the stories of the saints. I had visited other high crosses before, but recognized at once that this one, with its rich brown hue, was especially grand. Even though the images on this cross were worn down by the elements, a scene of two men holding each other caught my eye as I slowly circled the cross.

"My God!" I said aloud in excitement as I recognized the figures. "They are the desert fathers, Antony and Paul!" I knew already from my study of the Celi De reformers, who loved the desert Christians, that these two elders were frequently portrayed on the high crosses of Ireland. I didn't know, however, that I'd find this familiar scene on the Durrow cross. Nor did I have any expectation at what that story in stone would evoke in me. Immediately, out of the blue, I remembered my father's and my embrace before he left our house in St. Paul for the last time.

Standing there at the foot of the high cross and staring up at the scene of Antony and Paul, I realized why I had always been drawn to that story by St. Jerome. It was the story of Dad and me, of our relationship! Like the two desert fathers, we had spent a lifetime searching for each other. For years, there seemed to have been a great silence between us, a dread darkness, a vast desert caused by what I thought were different personalities, perspectives, expectations. Only shortly before Dad died had we finally experienced, without our defenses up, how much we meant to each other.

Something else came to me as I stood in the midst of the ancient tombstones in front of the high cross. My weeks of grieving were teaching me that all the time I thought we were so different, we were actually very much alike. Perhaps that had been the problem all along. Both of us were passionate in our convictions. Both of us could be very persistent. Ah, yes, that had been the source of our major conflicts; both of us could be stubborn when we chose to be.

If that was the cause of our disagreements, though, what ultimately counted was that, before Dad died, we had reached a new and deeper level of reconciliation. We had, like Antony and Paul, shared bread together during those last days at our house before Dad left; we too had shared a last embrace. I suddenly remembered the presence of the crow in the story of the two desert elders. Like the young crow outside my window, it too had announced the older man's approaching death. But, I reminded myself, it had also acted in the elders' story as a bringer of communion. The crow, a symbol of death, was doing the same for me. It was revealing the paradox of intimate, loving friendships, that through death, communion with another is not necessarily lost at all, but strengthened, deepened, integrated into the center of a person's being, heart, and soul.

I stared up at the scene of those two men in each other's arms and felt strangely comforted. In some mysterious way, I thought, the death of my father and my resulting grief was bringing me even closer to Dad than when he was alive. I was experiencing, more than ever before, a new level of communion with him. The bitter taste of grief was slowly, painfully being transformed, like Columcille's apples. It was not the absence or alleviation of that inner anguish so much as the distillation of it into something uniquely different, an experience of deep joy that at least for the moment transcended grief and guilt. I knew, however, that I had yet to see, as Antony did with Paul, my father's shining face.

I drove on to Maynooth, where in 1988 I had taught a course in spirituality and used the library for my research. At the gate-house, I phoned two faculty members who, as friends and mentors, had helped me over the years with my writing. Ronan Drury, I was told, was away, but Enda McDonagh invited me to have dinner in the dining room with him and the other priests. I was extremely happy to be back at Maynooth, and, considering the tiring day on the road, to be the recipient again of Irish hospitality. I slept that night in a bed on the second floor of the main building, with a window overlooking the front gate and the ruins of a medieval castle.

The next morning, after breakfast, I joined Enda in the sacristy. He had earlier offered to celebrate a Mass for my father. While he was vesting, he asked if I would like to act as a server. I happily agreed, though it had been years since I'd served at Mass. We processed together to one of the side altars, and the liturgy began. I felt very much at home there, surrounded by reminders of my Irish heritage: the windows with their stories in stained glass, the wallpaper with its green shamrocks intertwined. I was suddenly startled from my reverie, however, when I heard Enda ask God in his opening prayers, "Forgive us too for all those things which we now regret, especially concerning our parents."

I couldn't believe my ears. "He knows!" I said to myself in surprise. "Even though I have not told him of my feelings of remorse and of guilt!" As the ancient ritual of the Mass continued, I thought of Peter O'Dwyer's tears in Kinsale and those of the old man in the pub. You can tell those who know, I thought. They have experienced grief, and from it learned compassion.

CHAPTER IX

The Face in the Mirror

In a certain sense, we become our own father
when, through a good disposition of our soul, we
shall have formed and engendered ourselves and
have brought ourselves to the light.
——Gregory of Nyssa

SUNDAY, AUGUST 18, THE DAY FOLLOWING the Mass at
Maynooth with Enda, I flew into Heathrow Airport outside
London. As I waited for a bus to Oxford, I recalled the phone
conversation that I had had when I called home the night
before. I had spoken briefly with JoAnne and John; Daniel was
outside playing. JoAnne told me that she had been in touch
with my mother, who was "doing as well as can be expected."
When I asked how she and our sons were, she replied, "I'm
fine, and so are the boys, except for occasional tears. Daniel
usually has a good cry every night before he falls asleep. John,
of course, is less demonstrative."

"Well, another week, and I'll be home," I told her. "You were
right to encourage me to go. This trip has not only been helpful
for my research, but for the grieving I need to do. Thank you.
And thank you for caring for the boys while I'm away."

John came on the line next. "How are you, John?" I asked.

"I'm ok," he replied, "but I miss Grandpa Ed so much. And
I miss you, too, Daddy. When are you coming home?"

"In another week; it won't be long. Then you and Dan and
I can go up to see Grandma."

"Yes, I want to."

"Help your mother, and I'll see you soon," I told him, and then added, "I love you, John."

"I love you too, Daddy."

On the bus ride to Oxford that afternoon, I savored John's last words to me. It meant a great deal to me to hear him say that he loved me. In my grief I had begun to recognize certain traits that he shared with me. He too was close to his mother; he too had a younger brother whom his father seemed to favor; he too seemed hesitant in expressing his feelings to his dad. When I returned, I was determined to show him that I loved him as much as I loved my second son. I remembered a conversation with Daniel sometime before. "Dad," Dan had asked me, "do you love John or me more?" I answered truthfully, "I love you both with all my heart; there's no room to love either of you more—or less." I wanted both of them to know that, although a father's love may be expressed differently, his love is constant.

As the bus crossed the bridge into the city, I saw Magdalen College's cream-colored tower and spires rising above the trees. A deep sense of happiness filled my being. Three years before, I had stayed at the St. Theosevia Center of Christian Spirituality and, during that time, had learned a great deal from my studies about the spirituality of the desert and Celtic Christians. The effect the city and people had had on me personally, however, was even more profound. I had come there, encumbered with baggage from the vicissitudes of midlife, and found the city, to quote C. S. Lewis, "a place of loosening chains." Now I was back, carrying a different sort of bundle on my back, filled with grief, regret, and the anguish of loss.

A cab driver took me to St. Theosevia's on Canterbury Road, only minutes from the center of Oxford, where I found Donald Allchin waiting for me. He hadn't changed since my last brief visit there a year before, when I had been passing through on my way to Scotland and Cornwall. I had dreamed about him shortly after my father's death, and now as I hugged him close, I realized that he had become, without my being conscious of it, a spiritual father to me. Thomas Merton may have brought us together, but Donald was now my mentor in the flesh. He had taught me a great deal about Celtic spirituality, and I admired his lifetime commitment to ecumenism, especially among Anglican, Roman Catholic, and Eastern Orthodox churches. I had learned much by just living with him, as the early desert father Antony had done with his mentors before he journeyed to see Paul. Donald had introduced me to all sorts of scholars and ordinary people intensely interested in the history of the Celtic churches. He was the one who had "nudged" me into recovering my belief in angels, telling me to "let the angels guide you." Through the synchronicity I had experienced at that time, they had! Donald also had introduced me to his good friend, Sister Benedicta Ward, a member of the theology faculty at the University of Oxford and a scholar in medieval history. Years before I met her, Benedicta's writings on the desert Christians had broadened my interest in the world of the desert elders. In the fall of 1988 she too had mentored me when I met with her each week to discuss my latest research.

Donald and I went out for supper the evening I arrived. He took me to his favorite Chinese restaurant, and we caught up on each other's lives and the international state of ecumenism. Both of us agreed that, institutionally, ecumenism was not doing very well between the Roman Catholic and Anglican churches, but that progress continued at the grass roots.

When I told him of my father's sudden death, he responded immediately with sympathy. His parents, he said, had been dead for some time. "You're never the same after they're gone," he said with sadness in his voice, "yet they seem closer to me now than when they were alive." We walked together after our meal back along Broad Street, past the Bridge of Sighs, the Bodleian Library, and the Sheldonian with its rows of wonderful Greek and Roman faces lit by the last rays of the setting sun. I went up to my room when we got back to do some reading before turning out the light.

I awoke early the next morning and quietly stole down the steps to the kitchen for a cup of coffee and some toast. The patristic conference at which I was to deliver my paper on Cassian was not to start until that night, so I intended to make the most of my day. I took a quick shower, dressed, and went out. The familiar streets were just beginning to come alive, and as I walked toward the center of Oxford, I stopped along the way to hike through the large park across from Keble College with its tall oaks and stately evergreens. Then, when Blackwells Bookstore opened on Broad Street, I happily entered and perused its shelves for the remainder of the morning. At a pub next door I had a bowl of hot pea soup and a dry ham sandwich for lunch, then boarded a bus out to Fairacres where the Convent of the Incarnation is located. I had visited this Anglican community, the Sisters of Love of God, on other occasions, primarily to see Sister Helen, a tiny woman in her late sixties who shared with me a love of Celtic saints.

I rang the bell. One of the younger nuns answered the door and, when I asked for Sister Helen, showed me to the visitors' parlor. Within minutes Sister Helen appeared, smiling warmly and carrying a tray with a tea set, pieces of chocolate cake, and an assortment of shortbreads. As a member of this contemplative community, she wore a traditional habit: a black veil and a long brown woolen habit with a bronze Jerusalem cross hanging from her neck. She put the tray down on a table, and we hugged each other affectionately.

"Well, it's good to see you again, Edward," she said, then inquired, "Would you like some tea? I just brewed it."

I assented readily but declined the sweets since I had just eaten. She poured me a cup and, as she handed it to me, asked, "How was your trip to Ireland?"

I quickly told her how well it had gone, considering the circumstances. Although I had written that I would be coming to Oxford, she was not aware that my father had died shortly before I left. Now I told her of his death and of its aftermath. "I am feeling so filled with regret," I said, my voice breaking with emotion. "What I keep remembering is our fights, and how long it took for me finally to become a more loving son."

Sister Helen sat forward in her chair, her face immediately showing her compassion. "Oh, Edward," she responded, "it was the same with my mother and me. She did not die suddenly as your father did, but lingered on. I visited her often—this was before I entered the convent—and I tried to make things easier for her. I think I did, and I think she appreciated it." She paused and took a sip from her cup. "And yet," she continued, putting down the cup, "when she died, I felt horrible."

I could tell from Sister Helen's tone of voice that she still had some sense of regret, even years later.

"But I think now," she said, recovering her composure, "that that goes with loving someone. I have discovered that I was not the only one to feel that way. It seems to be part of the human condition that, no matter how good our relationship with our parents has been, we often feel guilty after their deaths—the guilt of thinking we could have or should have done better." Then looking me straight in the eyes, she added, "I have never met a person who does not have some feelings of guilt when a parent dies. Somehow, no matter how loving or attentive we've been while they were alive, we blame ourselves or wish we had done things differently."

I was moved by her honesty and willingness to talk about her own life. Those qualities seemed to give me the courage to acknowledge even more what was happening within me.

"But it's not only guilt and regret that I feel," I told her. "I also wonder whether I brought about Dad's death!"

She stared at me. "What do you mean?"

I explained my fears that through my prayers I was somehow responsible for my father's sudden death. "I just don't know," I said, "but it's the most horrible kind of emptiness and guilt."

Sister Helen leaned over, took my hands in hers, and said with conviction, "You were not responsible, Edward. God would not act solely on any one prayer. Somehow, for some reason, it was just time for your father to die." I began to cry again, and she paused, and then said gently, but emphatically, "It's the child in you, the part of every person that wants to take responsibility for everything, and blames itself for what the parents do. You didn't cause your father's death, but the child within you wants to take the blame in order to somehow make sense of it all."

Tears flowed down my face at her words. I cried for my father, wanting him back again. I cried for forgiveness—whether I was responsible or not. I cried in gratitude for her acceptance.

Sister Helen handed me a tissue box. "Tears and grief will come," she said, "especially when you are tired and feeling lonely. The child within is crying for his lost father. You need to respect this child, listen to him, welcome him, and give him comfort when he's been left, it seems, out in the cold." As I wiped my eyes and blew my nose, she continued to advise me. "I can tell that you're still in a state of shock. But let me assure you of one thing. You will find your father again—at that deep level which is beyond articulation. It will come to you, simply as a knowing. In your heart you will know that your father is part of that communion of saints that both of us believe in so passionately."

I knew what she was talking about. I already had had intimations of it.

I left her, waving good-bye at the door of the convent, a small fragile figure, yet powerful with the strength of her convictions. "A wise confessor, like St. Ita of Ireland," I thought, as I climbed aboard the red double-decker bus that would take me back to Oxford and St. Theosevia's.

Over dinner at the Randolph Hotel later that evening, I told Sister Benedicta about my talk with Sister Helen. We had come there following the formal tea that opened the patristics conference on the grounds of Christ Church. "I lied at my father's funeral," I told her, "telling everyone that I had no regrets. I am still filled with them, with memories of fights I wish we hadn't had and of harsh words I wish I hadn't spoken. But, at least now, I don't feel responsible for his death. That has been a major consolation."

The next day, August 20, four weeks to the day after my father breathed his last, I stood at a podium in the building where Oxford University students take their exams each year—and where C. S. Lewis used to lecture. One of the dons, dressed in his black academic garb, introduced me to those who had gathered to hear my talk on John Cassian. The long, narrow room was crowded. I noticed some familiar faces, although most were scholars and people whom I had never seen before. Donald was there, and Benedicta. I appreciated the moral support they offered by their presence. I began my talk by dedicating it to my father who, I told the assembly, had died a short time before. "Like the desert fathers," I said, "he too taught more by example than words." The room was suddenly quiet.

I proceeded with my talk, telling the audience the story of the two friends, John Cassian and Germanus, and their visit to the holy places of Palestine about 380 C.E. In Bethlehem they had joined a monastery near the cave of the Nativity; they remained there, sharing a common cell. After a few years they moved on to Egypt, where for the next fifteen years they lived with various desert solitaires. What drew them to the desert regions, I said, was their longing to learn the rules of the spiritual life from those mature and spiritually wise teachers whom Cassian called the elders. I went on to describe what the two friends had learned from the desert elders: the importance of having a teacher, spiritual guide, or soul friend; and how God's guidance and wisdom come most often through human mediation, especially, as Cassian says, through the "experience," "sure example," and "spirit" of the elders. Leadership itself, according to Cassian, depends upon an apprenticeship with a more experienced person who teaches the importance of self-disclosure, of honesty, of paying attention to our experiences and what we might learn from them. All of this can be learned through some form of structured training program, as found in Cassian's description of the monastic communities in the desert of his day. Most often, however, it is learned simply by living with an elder for a time. These people provide, Cassian says, a model of authentic spirituality and of the holy life.

As I read the paper on Cassian, looking up intermittently from the text to establish eye contact with my listeners, I became aware of how truly wise Cassian was. I thought of Donald, and how much I had learned from him by spending my days at St. Theosevia's in his company. I remembered the hours with Benedicta, and how quickly the time had flown when we were discussing our mutual passion for history. I recalled Helen's sound advice to study spirituality not only as it is written about in books but as it is expressed through music, prayer, and landscape. Most recently, she had modeled for me what Cassian calls a compassionate listener, being willing to share her own story in a ministry of reconciliation. Such disclosures, Cassian says, can be truly educative. Not only can they intellectually benefit people who may be younger or less experienced than ourselves, but they actually can bring about healing through our openness and honesty. Self-disclosure helps us discover that we are not alone in our struggles; as a result, we are given hope. That had been my experience with Helen the day before; that was my experience through my loving relationships with my wife, my sons, my family, Benedicta, Donald, and other friends. They were all giving me the strength to carry on in the midst of grieving.

I told the audience that Cassian recommends that everything arising in the heart be shared with the elders, for anything that lies within us sheds its destructive power when it is brought into the light. The elder's responsibility in receiving another's confession is to listen without judgment; as one of the holy men wisely told Cassian, "not only must we not denounce the fault which someone has admitted, but we must avoid despising any pain, however slight." With such compassion and deep respect for another's suffering, the elders act, Cassian says, as a kind of glass or mirror by which the younger monks "learn both the causes of the sins by which they are troubled and the remedies for them." In this way the elders minister to their proteges as "true physicians of the soul."

I believed all this, for it had happened to me—not just with Sister Helen, but on numerous other occasions with trusted friends or spiritual guides. Only open and honest confession had set me free, had helped heal me of my brokenness and sin, had allowed me to get on with my life. Christianity has always maintained this, I knew from my study of the history of Christian spirituality; my work with recovering alcoholics and their families confirmed its value. Cassian is simply saying, I told my audience, that confession to a reliable guide on a regular basis is good for the body and for the soul.

Cassian also maintains that the recipient of someone else's mentoring is likely to become a mentor to others, sharing his or her experience with them in relationships that are reciprocal. Judging from what Cassian wrote, one of the most important roles for any elder, mentor, or spiritual leader is being someone who inspires in others the confidence to pursue their own goals and dreams. This role of exemplar cannot be defined easily, nor is it something that anyone achieves through personal effort. It seems, quite simply, related to teaching more by example than words.

I had started my talk with a reference to my father, and as I reached this section on the role of the exemplar, the memory of Dad and his tremendous influence upon me was reinforced by Cassian's insights. My life, I knew, had been graced with many mentors who had taught me much about the true purpose of life, love, and about life's final goal, union with God. But, of all those mentors it was my parents who had had the greatest influence. They were my first and most significant exemplars. Through their love, and, yes, their human failures at loving, they taught me as no one else could about the need to love and the need to seek forgiveness. Like mirrors, they had reflected back to me the great reality: there is a loving, compassionate God who is always willing to forgive, and who has, in fact, forgiven us before we even recognize the need to ask.

In particular Dad, throughout his life and now even more so with his dying, mirrored fatherhood to me. By my constant recalling over the past weeks his relationship with me, and mine with him, I was coming to new awarenesses of my own fatherhood, of my need to choose what sort of father I wanted to be to my sons. My grief was teaching me, through memories of my father, what I should do and what I should try to avoid doing, which values and practices I hoped to pass on to my sons and which ones I hoped not to repeat. If Dad had difficulty in saying "I love you" to me, I now realized the need for me to say more frequently those very words to my own sons. If he was reticent in acknowledging errors or asking for forgiveness, possibly out of fear of losing his "authority" with his children, I needed more often to admit when I made mistakes, to say, "I'm sorry." Grieving was initiating me into fatherhood, *my* fatherhood.

I was learning all this from my father and from the fathers of the desert too—not only about my call to fatherhood but to the broader vocation of becoming a *spiritual* father: someone who freely loves others without expectations, without any explicit or implicit demands; who loves others more compassionately and more freely for who they are in the sight of God rather than for whom we may want them to be; someone who affirms and facilitates in another person his or her unique way to God. Spiritual fatherhood depends upon the acceptance and integration of both paternal and maternal heritages, for to be an effective parent or spiritual guide presupposes the acceptance of both the masculine and feminine sides that our parents personify. To deny one of them is to fail to integrate fully the two within, to be cut off from the living springs of our spiritual roots.

Most of all, I was learning that, like my father, my other mentors, and the desert Christians themselves, my call to fatherhood on a daily basis is frequently to teach more by example than words, to become as welcoming and forgiving as my father was to me.

I concluded the reading of my paper by suggesting that I thought the core of Cassian's spirituality was his appreciation of friendship and its enduring bonds: "After all, it was Cassian's friendship with Germanus that perhaps first gave him the courage to embark on his adventure into the desert regions. It was the friendship provided by the desert elders that taught them both so much about the God of fire who transforms minds and hearts. It is the stories Cassian tells that remind us of how much our own elders and wisdom figures have changed our lives by their acceptance, love, and inspiration." I had known all of this before my father's death, but now that belief had been strengthened immeasurably by my experience of grieving.

The rest of the week at Oxford flew by as I went from one lecture to another. It was the same week the Russian communists attempted to overthrow Gorbachev, an event that caused a great deal of anxiety and turmoil worldwide. In between the academic presentations, I would duck into a coffee shop across the street from the Exams Building, sip coffee, and read about the latest events. I was very concerned about the future of Russia and uneasy over international repercussions. So far from home and my own family, I increasingly wanted to be safely back with them and not on the other side of the Atlantic. By Friday morning and the end of the conference, I was ready to leave for London, where I planned to stay before leaving for the States on Sunday.

It was pouring rain when I climbed aboard the bus with my briefcase, suitcase, and assorted items. I settled in the front seat, behind the driver, hoping to enjoy the scenery and passing countryside. There was not, however, a lot to see, with the rain falling in torrents. When we arrived in London, the driver dropped me off on a street not far from Victoria Station. I had an umbrella with me, but with my hands full of luggage, it was virtually useless against the wind and the rain. By the time I arrived at the Enrico Hotel, I was soaked to the skin. I checked in at the desk downstairs, happy, despite the weather, to be back at a place where I had stayed many times before. It is not a large or expensive hotel, but it is clean and offers tourists a better breakfast of bacon, eggs, and fried toast than anywhere else.

I took my things up to the room assigned to me at the top of the third-floor stairs, across from three communal bathrooms. I knew immediately that this was less than an ideal location; with the paper-thin walls of each room, I would hear everyone coming up to that floor, as well as the flush of toilets at all hours. I had no choice in the matter, however, for all the rooms were full. Resigned to little sleep at night, I took a shower, put on dry clothes, and headed for the Tate Gallery, about a twenty-minute walk from Enrico's. I went there with a specific purpose in mind. I wanted to see Stanley Spencer's "Resurrection, Cookham." I had seen the huge painting on a previous visit and been struck by its scene of a churchyard with heroes of both Hebrew and Christian traditions as well as ordinary people rising from their graves. I wanted to see it again, to take in, with my eyes and my soul, its vibrant colors, its dark, green landscape, and the hope of resurrection that it portrayed.

Clutching my umbrella against the gusts of wind, I recalled what I had read about Spencer and the painting. He had been inspired to set the resurrection in the churchyard at Cookham, the small town where he was born and raised, by a phrase of John Donne's in which the poet describes a churchyard as being "the holy suburb of Heaven." Many of Spencer's paintings, including the ones with explicitly religious subjects, are set in the familiar places of his childhood. For him, religious feelings fused with the hearth, the home, what he called "the Domestic." He once said that the village of Cookham was part of the church as much as the church was part of the village, and it was there that he had found his spiritual way. Spencer considered the cemetery as the spiritual heart of the town where one's ancestors and mentors lay buried, but only temporarily. He believed the mystery of the resurrection to be "the meeting of two worlds, this world and the resurrected-life world." The figures in his paintings of the resurrection, including the one at Cookham, are thus portrayed as filled with awe and happiness, rubbing and stretching their limbs and embracing their loved ones once again. Cemeteries, Spencer believed, were places of wonder, of great joy, of hope—despite the pain associated with death. This was, I thought, the meaning of resurrection—that evil and death are not the last word, and that God, goodness, and our love for one another will triumph in the end.

During his lifetime Spencer painted a variety of works on the resurrection theme, but the one inspired by Cookham is his most well-loved. As I remembered it, on the right-hand side of the painting, ranged along a white-and-tan church wall, are the great wisdom figures from the past, including Moses with a long, dark beard, looking like an Hasidic rabbi, carrying two stone tablets with the ten commandments engraved on them. He, along with others, possibly apostles, are dressed in white vestments and seem to be trying to adjust to their new state of life. At least two figures are covering their eyes from the rays of the morning sun, while others look around in amazement. At the center of the painting is the church's porch or portico, covered over with hanging white roses in full blossom. Under the portico God the Father stands, his hands reaching down to a seated, maternal-looking Christ, also dressed in white, cradling three children in his arms. Spencer, I recalled, had had his future wife Hilda pose for both Father and Son, because he wanted to emphasize the feminine, nurturing side of God. He was in continuity with the older medieval English tradition in which God was seen as having both masculine and feminine qualities. My favorite mystic, Julian of Norwich, had written centuries before, "As truly as God is our Father, so truly is God our Mother." And, of course, Jesus himself had used images in his storytelling that reflected his understanding of the feminine aspects of God: comparing God to a female householder searching for a lost coin (Lk 15:8-10) or to a bakerwoman kneading the leaven of the reign of God into the dough of this world (Mt 13:33). Jesus' own feminine side is manifest in his intimate relationships with women and in his comparison of himself to a mother hen who longs to cuddle her chicks under her wing (Mt 23:37).

Spencer was ahead of his time in his awarenesses, his theology. He was also a celebrant of the sacredness of the so-called ordinary. Throughout "Resurrection, Cookham" one finds ordinary people in various stages of dress and undress, seated, lying, or standing among shrubs, trees, flowers, and tombstones. A man and woman, fully clothed, and three of their children peek over the sides of one tomb, looking as if they do not know what to do next. A man climbs out of a grave with a clump of sunflowers on his back. Near him a young woman with daisies as her dress rises from a grave covered with the same flowers. Close to her, another couple, newly resurrected, hold notes in their hands. The woman seems to be reading to the man, possibly love poetry or something from her journal. In this section of the picture Spencer is said to have included portraits of his friends and family. The artist himself is depicted several times. In one place, toward the center of the painting, not far from the portico, he stands naked, leaning back on a gravestone, facing right. Kneeling close to him, facing left, is another naked male figure, a close friend of Spencer's who later became his brother-in-law. On the left side of the painting Hilda makes repeated appearances, just as Spencer does on the right. She is seen reclining, as if still asleep, on an ivy-covered tomb in the foreground of the painting, and, not far away, near a foot path, smelling a flower.

Spencer included more than relatives and friends, however, in "Resurrection, Cookham." Near Christ there is an entire section where a group of black women and men are rising from earth baked and cracked, apparently by the desert sun. They too look around in amazement. Spencer included them precisely because he believed that all cultures and creeds are part of this spiritual regeneration that Christians call resurrection. Even his idea of heaven was inclusive; as he saw it, heaven is "a kind of Jungle, but with all the people and animals on a love footing with each other."

As I climbed the long concrete steps outside the Tate Gallery, I knew why I loved Spencer's works, and "Resurrection, Cookham" in particular. He depicts ordinary people and the landscape in which they live as immersed in spirituality. Life, death, and resurrection make up a whole fabric; they are not separated one from the other. Significant too in "Resurrection, Cookham" is that, though God the Father and the Son are portrayed, the Holy Spirit is not. It is as if the artist is suggesting that the Spirit, unrepresented visually, pervades the entire scene with its vibrant figures and living landscape. While I wanted to see the painting in its entirety, I also was looking for one specific figure, found at the lower right of the picture. The figure is a man reclining in an open tomb, fully dressed in dark pants and a suitcoat. Spencer once said that this was a portrait of himself, depicting his state of "rest and contentment," "the shape of my soul." That psychic state of serenity was what I was now drawn to see.

I walked through the front doors and on toward that section of the gallery where his works are displayed. There on the walls before my eyes were Spencer's most striking paintings: the portraits of his wife and of himself, both naked, expressing his belief, like that of the ancient Greeks, that eros is intrinsically spiritual. There were also the "religious" scenes, including that of "St. Francis and the Birds," which, typical of

Spencer, contains not only wild birds, but farm animals, ducks, and chickens. St. Francis is portrayed as a corpulent figure, with a long white beard—looking more like Santa Claus than an ascetic. I stopped a moment to stare at him and thought immediately of Dad, because of his own love of birds. I remembered how Spencer himself had said that his idea of St. Francis was inspired by the memory of his dead father.

I resumed my search for "Resurrection, Cookham," my eyes scanning the gallery walls. It wasn't there! I could find only a huge empty space where it once had been. Thoroughly disappointed, I returned to the main desk in the lobby to inquire what had become of it. A young woman, aware of my agitation, told me politely, "I'm sorry, sir, but that is on exhibit in Liverpool." When I asked her when it would be returned, she said she didn't know, "perhaps in a year or two."

I left the Tate disgusted, and irritated further by the rain that continued to fall in buckets. I had so wanted to see the painting again, to have my belief in the resurrection strengthened by Spencer's powerful portrayal.

That night, alone in my tiny cubicle at Enrico's, I sat at the desk in front of a full mirror that was attached to the wall and wrote in my journal: "The pain is back once more. I cry and that helps for a while, but it's there—that constant stab of grief just below the surface, waiting to be touched by some memory or sight that reminds me of Dad."

The following morning, Saturday, I wanted to get an early start. I was awake anyway, having gotten little sleep, as expected. After breakfast I went upstairs, got my umbrella (just in case), and then left for a walking tour of London. I wanted to see Westminster Abbey once again, to visit the Poets' Corner where Chaucer and other famous writers are buried, and to browse in some bookstores. I also hoped to purchase a ticket in the theater district to the musical "Phantom of the Opera." My day went by quickly. I had a lunch of salad and spaghetti near the theater where "Phantom" was playing, having been lucky enough to get one of the last tickets to the performance that afternoon. I read in the newspaper that the Russian coup against Gorbachev had failed, and then headed for the musical. Seated midpoint in the theater, about ten rows back from the stage, I had a full view of everything. The entire show was fabulous, with wonderful music, staging, and beautiful costumes. The only distraction was an older, British woman sitting next to me, who—I soon learned—liked to hum along with the songs. Before the curtains opened she told me that she and her husband were celebrating their fiftieth wedding anniversary, reminding me, of course, of the one that my family would not.

I had a leisurely dinner in the theater district, stopped at two antiquarian bookstores, and returned to Enrico's about 10:00 p.m. I planned to retire early, anticipating the stress of the flight back the next morning. "I'm ready," I told myself as I closed the door to my room. "This trip has been good for my soul. But I've been gone long enough. I want to go home." I brushed my teeth, washed my face, and prepared to retire. First, though, I wanted to pray in thanksgiving for all that I had received on this journey, as well as for a safe flight back. I turned out the overhead light and sat at the desk facing the full mirror. Then I lit a candle in front of the small icon of Jesus that I had carried along with me on my travels. I don't know how long I sat there staring into the flickering flame.

At some point in my praying it seemed to me that my father, who had now been dead more than a month, was suddenly there with me. It was as if the room filled with his presence, a presence almost palpable, as vivid and as real as if he had just physically entered the room, spoken to me, or touched my shoulder. This sense of his presence, initially so intense, frightened me. Then, in the mirror directly in front of me, I saw Dad's face; in the darkness I saw the reflection of an older face, as I remembered his, touched with sorrow, and yet strangely illuminated by the candlelight. This face first seemed to frown at me, and then, as I continued to stare transfixed, smiled reassuringly. The entire experience lasted perhaps only a minute or two, but it was as if I had entered some sort of timeless state. Dad was there, I could see him frowning and then smiling at me, and then he was gone. The intensity of the experience, however, no matter how long it actually lasted, left its imprint. It seemed as if it were some sort of vision, and I felt both afraid and awed.

I sat there for a few minutes more, praying to God for understanding of what had just happened in my room, in the mirror. Soon serenity came over me. I crossed myself, got up from my chair, turned on the light, and looked around. It was the same room, but now it was empty of Dad. He had left, but not without saying good-bye.

I picked up my journal, sat down at the desk again, and began to write, hoping my writing might clarify what had just occurred. I still felt a great deal of ambivalence. The face in the mirror, in the dark and shadows, of course, was mine, and yet *not* mine. It was Dad's. It was how I remembered him: the frown that I had seen when I was a child and an adolescent, disapproving of me and my glasses, coming after me when I played the radio too loud, telling me that I'd grow up to be a bum, saying that he wished I weren't his son. There was also, however, the smile, the feature I had come to see more often as I matured; the smile in the picture of the two of us that I had looked for in the attic after my return from his funeral; the smile on his face when he held my own two sons in his arms; the smile I had seen that last visit before his stroke.

Those were the two impressions of him, and of his relationship with me, that appeared in the mirror. They reminded me of aspects of his fatherhood *and* of aspects of my own. I hoped, as I scribbled in my journal, that my own sons would see fewer frowns and more smiles on my face as they grew older.

The experience of the face in the mirror also reminded me that Dad, though dead, was still very much alive. He not only lived somewhere in the spiritual realm, where souls wait for the resurrection, but in me, in my depth, in my heart. He and I now lived, I realized, in what Cassian calls "one dwelling," for we had truly become deeper friends than ever before, soul friends. I remembered what Arnie Puetz had said to me before Dad's funeral, that I was beginning to look more like my dad. Not only had I inherited his looks and much of his personality, I thought, but I had received from him a tremendous spiritual heritage that would live on.

I came back to the original experience. Whatever happened, I knew that the sense of Dad's presence with me in the room was more than my imagination. So was the vision in the mirror. And while the first impression in the mirror was a stern, disapproving look, one that I associated with our conflicts, the second was the one that lingered in my mind. The full smile that I'd seen on his face so often behind the bar was the one that expressed Dad's love for all sorts of people, including me! I was especially grateful for it, and I knew intuitively that here in this room a significant corner had been turned. My grieving would certainly continue at some deep level for all my life on earth, but now I was assured that Dad's life endures. His love for me and my love for him are stronger than anything, including death.

His smiling face brought back to me the memory of our last embrace and the spilled cup of coffee. He was not angry with me. He laughed, and his laughter, despite my irritation, blessed us both with its warmth and spontaneity. Tears and laughter, that's what I remembered about him as I closed my journal. Tears and laughter—signs of great love. "JoAnne was right," I said aloud, recalling her words to me the day of the phone call that changed my life. "Dad and I did have a good relationship! Not perfect, but good. And it continues, despite the horrible feelings of grief."

Months later I found a statement by Joseph Campbell that named the experience that night in my room as the rain fell on London: "For the son who has grown really to know the father, the agonies of the ordeal are readily borne; the world is no longer a vale of tears but a bliss-yielding, perpetual manifestation of the Presence."

Epilogue

> First pray for the gift of tears, so that through sorrowing you may tame what is savage in your soul. And having confessed your transgressions to the Lord, you will obtain forgiveness.
> —Evagrius, the Solitaire

I DROVE BACK TO KENSAL WITH JOHN a few days after returning to St. Paul. Dan did not come with us; he was acting out his intense grief at day-care, and a return to Kensal now would be too much for him to bear. John sat next to me, quiet as usual, perhaps wary of his father's changing moods. I tried to initiate some discussion, but I was conscious of his reticence. I didn't want to push him too hard. Silence, I had come to realize, is not necessarily a sign that there is no love between people or that nothing is happening. Perhaps, I thought, John is like me when I was his age, not knowing what to say to his father. Or maybe he simply just doesn't care to talk. What I do know, I told myself, is that, while he may be silent, John is very much aware of what is going on. I remembered the first week after Daniel had been born. I had been playing happily with him, so proud of having another son. "John is watching you, Ed," my wife had told me, "pay attention to him too."

Driving the same route to Fargo that I had taken by myself in late July, I noticed, once we'd left the cities far behind, changes in the landscape. Harvest had already begun; hay was cut and stacked in the fields. The sunflowers had lost their bright hues of yellow and orange and were now dried and brown, waiting to be gathered. Much of the corn and wheat had also been cut, and many fields plowed. The wheat that still stood, heated by the sun, smelled like bread baking in an oven.

Outside of Alexandria the rolling hills flattened out, and the wide open skies of the prairie became more visible. Clouds floated lazily in the bright sunshine. As I drove past Fergus Falls, I was aware that my early opinion of the Dakota plains was changing along with the seasons and the landscape. What I had once disliked, and at times detested, I now perceived in its plainness and simplicity as great beauty. I recalled the many times I had jokingly told people how my parents had taken me into North Dakota against my will, and how I had tried to get away as soon as possible. Now I recognized that I had grown fond of the land, the fields of wheat and corn, the solitary view. I remembered too how often I had asked myself as a younger man why I had gotten the father that I had. Now, I knew that, like my changed perspective on the landscape, I got the father I needed most for my own path to holiness.

None of us really ever knows our parents, I thought, as I drove on. About the time many of us are interested in asking who they are, they are gone. The finality of death, however, has a way of putting life in perspective. Although I had always credited my mother with passing on to me an interest in theology and spirituality, that passion also came to me through the silent example of my father. Day in and day out he revealed, through his work and his many friendships, those values that he held dear. He was passing them on to me, and, through me and JoAnne, to his grandsons. I had come to see, as a result of my grieving, that Dad truly was like the desert elders, whom Helen Waddell describes as teaching more by their example than words: "Of the depth of their spiritual experience they had little to say: but their every action showed a standard of values that turns the world upside down. It was their humility, their gentleness, their heart-breaking courtesy that was the seal of their sanctity to their contemporaries." Dad followed the rule of those desert elders: to receive people with hospitality and send them away in peace. His was the type of unassuming leadership that builds communities.

I remembered him and those desert Christians as I passed Fargo, driving on toward Valley City and then Kensal. From what I knew about the desert in books that I'd read, I recognized the similarities between desert lands and Dakota prairies. Both have landscapes that stretch as far as the eye can see, where earth and sky meet at the horizon in distant unison. Both have climates that can be harsh and, at times, cruel, producing in the people a spirited resilience and an appreciation of hospitality. That's why the desert spiritual tradition reflected so much of my dad's story, as his expressed that of the desert elders. I hoped someday to visit the desert, to travel to where Antony, Paul, and Jesus had walked. I especially wanted to climb Mount Sinai, where Moses saw the burning bush, to do penance for the sins against my father and thus finally to make amends for things in our relationship for which I had been responsible. This ancient Christian practice, doing penance for one's sins, was highly recommended by both desert guides and Celtic soul friends as a way of experiencing peace with self and God.

Besides this practice, the desert and Celtic spiritual traditions affirmed the value of tears. They said that tears can have great power—tears of regret, of confession, of cleansing, of joy. I was learning that now. I was learning, slowly and painfully, what they knew already: the desert itself is a metaphor, a symbol of the darkness that enters each of our lives at some point. With the help of God and of our friends, however, this entrance into the land of tears can be endured, can become, as painful as it is, a passage into light. From that passage we can learn a compassion that comes through sorrow, a wisdom that comes through tears. We begin to see that rather than running from our grief, we need to face it, acknowledge it, give it expression. Grieving is the price we pay for loving others, and the more deeply we love, the more we will grieve. Grieving provides us the opportunity to accept that a person is actually gone and to incorporate into our own spirit the spirit of another. It offers us the chance to learn to forgive them *and* ourselves, something not accomplished by our own effort but given through the acceptance and love of others.

I thanked God for the presence of love in my life: the love mirrored in the love of my parents and grandparents for me; the love from JoAnne that has transformed my life; the love of my sons, friends, and relatives, which keeps revealing to me the height, depth, and breadth of God's love. On the road—through Kensal, Springfield, New Harmony, Dublin, Skellig Michael, Oxford, and London—I had come to a little more acceptance of myself. I was genuinely sorry for the bitter fights and harsh words between me and my father, but I also realized now that my fights with Dad were a natural aspect of our being so much alike and, perhaps most of all, of our wanting *so much* to be loved and respected by the other.

In my grieving I was also coming to recognize that every son needs to separate himself from his father's expectations of him. It is natural for sons to fight with their fathers in order to forge their own identities. In some ways the fights I had with Dad, I thought, were perhaps necessary, as those with my sons will be. I had come to see in my wandering that, along with forgiveness, in every relationship of depth something fierce lies just below the surface. Anger is not necessarily a sign of rejection, but perhaps of intense love. When expressed, it can prick the boil, clear the air. Though it took so long—a lifetime, really—for Dad and me to recognize finally how much we loved each other, it was comforting to know that we did, at last, come to that realization, standing together under the lilac bushes in the backyard. I was especially grateful to God that our last words to each other had been "I love you."

By the time John and I reached Kensal and saw the sign, with its letters neatly painted, welcoming us, I was thoroughly tired of the road. It seemed as if I had been travelling ever since my father's stroke—and I now concluded that indeed I had. Such wandering, my own Celtic ancestors knew, can be good for the soul. For me, these travels had become a form of pilgrimage.

I drove across the railroad tracks that had brought my grandparents as newly-weds to this town in the first days of the twentieth century, turned left at the corner by the rental home for the elderly, and a few blocks further took a right up the gravel drive. As I got out of the car, I noticed that in the front yard the dark tire marks were still plainly visible from the site of Dad's and my last battle.

Mom greeted John and me at the door, obviously happy to see us once again. She had aged dramatically over the past month, with new creases in her forehead and lines around her eyes. Her grieving had only intensified. Still, she smiled and hugged each of us close. "It's so good to see you again," she said. I responded, "It seems like years since I was last here—and only yesterday." I walked with her and John across the back deck where we had had so many good times.

Later that afternoon Dale and Marybeth arrived from Fargo, planning to stay the weekend. It was the first time in years that the three of us were at home without our spouses. It felt right that we should be with Mom. I also sensed that in some mysterious way Dad's death was bringing us closer, making us less judgmental of each other's faults, more accepting of our vulnerabilities. Mom brought out the sympathy cards that she had received, over five hundred in all. We took turns passing them around and reading them. I was amazed at how many lives Dad and Mom had touched. Personal messages on the cards frequently referred to my father's humor, generosity, and, not surprisingly, his hospitality. I fell asleep in the chair, exhausted from my travels and overcome, once again, by my grief.

When I awoke from my nap, I walked over to the window in the living room and stared out at the lawn and trees. Turning away, I noticed the two plants that Mom had placed on the table to catch the fading light. One was a shamrock, its tiny white flowers and green leaves lush and full; the other was a rugged-looking cactus, dark green, with sharp thorns. The latter too, however, at this time of year had flowers in bloom, large and shapely, in bright reddish shades, like tongues of fire. These plants reminded me of the two spiritual traditions that I love, one of which valued education, books, and words, and the other silence, solitude, and listening. As I looked upon them, I realized how much they represented my parents, their different personalities and differing ways of mentoring me. While pride of place, in my heart, had always gone to the shamrock, I knew now the inherent beauty of the cactus, despite its thorns and its potential for causing pain.

That evening Mom and I walked out to the cemetery alone. A gentle breeze made walking pleasant. Mom seemed anxious to talk about the last month and all that had happened so suddenly. I listened. I was determined to support her in her agony.

"How can I live without him?" she asked just as we reached the outskirts of town. "Norma told me on the way back from Fargo that, 'if one of you had to go, it's good that Ed went first, Elaine, for he couldn't have lived very long without you.'"

"I think Norma's right, Mom," I replied. "Dad wouldn't have been able to do much on his own. But you can, Mom, and we want you to take care of yourself. We all need you now more than ever."

I was genuinely concerned about her. C. S. Lewis had written that grief is like fear. I felt that for my mother. I was afraid for her, and for all of us if anything should happen to her. The months ahead would prove the wisdom of JoAnne's words to me when I told her that my father was dead: "It's going to be very hard for your mother, living without your dad. It was obvious how much the two of them loved each other."

"I know I shouldn't say this," Mom continued, "but I wish I had died with him. Why didn't I? If he was going to have a stroke that day, why didn't he have it in the car on way to the clinic? Then we both could have died." Her voice trailed off into silence. She seemed both relieved at having said what she felt and guilty for having those feelings. "Why did he have to die?" she asked when I took her hand in mine. "Why weren't we given one more year, so we could have celebrated our fiftieth anniversary as a family? Why now when he had just begun to enjoy his retirement?"

I did not have answers to any of those questions. Nor could I answer the one behind all of them: Why have I been left alone?

We walked together past the fields of cut wheat, bailed hay, and drying sunflowers to the cemetery gates, then down the road, past my grandparents' tombstone, to the new grave. There was not yet any marker. The only thing visible on the mound of brown earth was a wooden stick with a multicolored plastic pinwheel that my sister had planted earlier that day. The prairie wind blew it first one direction then another, twirling the bright colors of red, blue, and green, reflecting the rays of the setting sun.

We stood there in the middle of the graves and prayed for my father. My mother cried once more, whispering at one point, "The hardest thing of all is knowing that I'll never see him again."

Standing there, I realized that I had been initiated into the great mysteries—those of life and of death, of light and of darkness. I had watched my two sons being born and my father die, had seen the first intake of breath and the last exhalation. Our lives are surrounded by mystery and immersed in its depths. I thought of the graves in Springfield, where Lincoln's body had been placed, and the bouquet of flowers at Ardmore, Ireland, with the words "We miss you, Grandpa." I remembered the cemetery at Ballinskelligs where I learned about the universality of grief, and the cross at Durrow where the two desert fathers, Antony and Paul, had embraced with a love that transcended death. I knew now that God was even more mysterious than I had ever imagined. Seeking God, I had entered the seminary when I was very young. Years later I had arrived at this: No words can ultimately express the mystery of God. Somehow only paradox gives us intimations of that Reality—the paradox of autumn when everything is dying and everything is ripe. If we resort to words, perhaps Paul's to Antony are the closest we can come: "Behold, God has sent us our dinner, God the merciful, God the compassionate."

I knew, then, that death for me was no longer a frightening reality, for my father would be there waiting for me on the other side. Of course, I believed in the communion of saints before this all happened, but now I knew that, along with my grandparents, Dad would also give me support in my own passage to light, waiting, as he always did, to welcome me home.

I remembered the elusive painting by Spencer, and the artist's statement that the cemetery at Cookham was, for him, "the spiritual heart of the town." "This is where my loved ones lie," I thought to myself, "Dad, Grandma Mary, Grandpa John. This is my holy ground where the bodies of those who live in my heart and soul await the resurrection."

Walking back to town along the same road, Mom and I said almost nothing at all, too drained of energy, too tired by the awareness of our loss and of our sadness. Then suddenly both of us stopped, transfixed by the wonder of the western sky lit up at dusk by the last rays of the setting sun. There, across the open fields, we saw what appeared to be a giant mural, painted in the sky with broad strokes. One part of the sky glowed with reds and oranges, while another shone with varying shades of blue. At the center was a particularly bright circle. We took turns pointing out the different aspects of this colorful portrait, one that in its entirety seemed to show a scene of a lake with trees bordering the shore. Each of us thought the same thing. Mom was the one to give it voice: "It's Dad."

"It's the most extraordinary sunset I've ever seen," I said.

We continued gazing at this natural scene of serenity. I thought of the birds in the cemetery at Dad's burial, and then of the crow outside my window before Dad's death. Nature itself seems to announce and recognize the passing of good people. Stories from the gospels and the lives of the saints came to mind: the eclipse of the sun and the darkness that covered the land when Jesus died (Lk 23:44); the two moons and a star that appeared at the death of the Celtic woman Samthann, convincing a certain abbot-friend that she had indeed entered heaven; the raging storms and seas off the Scottish island of Iona that calmed mysteriously when St. Columcille was laid to rest.

Desert Christians too understood the intercommunion of humanity and the natural world. They also told stories of animals that appeared at the time of death: a lion helped the monk Zossima bury the desert mother Mary of Egypt, while other lions with "their manes flying" came to help Antony bury Paul. Then, of course, there is the story of a certain philosopher, evidently a book lover like me, who came to visit the desert father Antony. He asked, "Father, how can you be so happy when you are deprived of the consolation of books?" Antony replied: "My book, O philosopher, is the nature of created things. Any time I want to read the words of God, the book is before me."

That night, sleeping in the bed where my grandfather and I had slept when I was a child, I dreamed that Dad was back, sitting on the deck with Mom and me. In the dream, I am filled with gratitude at our reunion, that he's somehow been brought back from the dead. I look at him with love. He says nothing but seems happy, at ease, at home, smiling at me, through his tears.

I was awakened from the dream by the wind and the scratching of tree branches against the side of the house. At the first streaks of light across the open prairie skies, I heard the birds chirping, their music welcoming the dawn.

Works Cited

Campbell, Joseph. *The Hero With a Thousand Faces*. Princeton, NJ: Princeton University Press, 1973.

Gibson, Edgar, trans. "The Conferences of John Cassian." In P. Schaff and H. Wace, eds., *Nicene and Post-Nicene Fathers of the Christian Church*, Vol. 11 (Grand Rapids, MI: Wm. B. Eerdmans, 1986).

_____. "The Institutes of John Cassian." In P. Schaff and H. Wace, eds., *Nicene and Post-Nicene Fathers of the Christian Church*, Vol. 11 (Grand Rapids, MI: Wm. B. Eerdmans, 1986).

Hausherr, Irenee. *Spiritual Direction in the Early Christian East*. Kalamazoo, MI: Cistercian Publications, 1990.

Luibheid, Colm. *John Cassian: Conferences*. New York: Paulist Press, 1985.

Merton, Thomas. *The Wisdom of the Desert*. New York: New Directions, 1970.

Palmer, G.E.H., Philip Sherrard, and Kallistos Ware, eds. *The Philokalia*, Vol. 1. London: Faber & Faber, 1979.

Power, Rev. P. *Life of St. Declan of Ardmore*. London: Irish Texts Society, 1914.

Russell, Norman, trans. *The Lives of the Desert Fathers*. Kalamazoo, MI: Cistercian Publications, 1981.

Sellner, Edward. *Wisdom of the Celtic Saints*. Notre Dame, IN: Ave Maria Press, 1993.

Stokes, Whitley. *The Martyrology of Oengus the Culdee*. London, 1905.

Waddell, Helen. *Songs of the Wandering Scholars*. London: The Folio Society, 1982.

_____. *The Desert Fathers*. Ann Arbor, MI: University of Michigan Press, 1972.

Ward, Benedicta, trans. *The Sayings of the Desert Fathers*. Kalamazoo, MI: Cistercian Publications, 1975.

_____. *The Desert of the Heart*. London: Darton, Longman & Todd, 1988.